Praise for *Why You'll Never Find the One*

"This book is a warm hug of encouragement and understanding for anyone feeling unlucky in love. Akinterinwa's insightful and logical commentary on dating paired with her on-point cartoons creates a captivating and much-needed dating pep talk."
—**GABI CONTI**, author of *Twenty Guys You Date in Your Twenties* and creator of the podcast *Am I Dating a Serial Killer?*

"*Why You'll Never Find the One* is a wise, funny guidebook that will be your companion through the indignities of the dating scene—while quietly showing you the way to fall in love with yourself. Sarah Akinterinwa's insightful words and delightful drawings get to the heart of what it's like to be single and endlessly searching. They will show you that you're not alone in this journey."
—**LIANA FINCK**, *New Yorker* cartoonist and author of *Let There Be Light*

"Sarah Akinterinwa's kind, clear-eyed book should be pressed into the hands of any young person who feels defeated by dating in our digital age."
—**BLYTHE ROBERSON**, author of *How to Date Men When You Hate Men*

"I love Sarah's voice—a wry wit that pairs well with a clean drawing style. In her new book, she treats us to her cartoon people and their humorous outlook on life, and in the process passes along some very sage advice about being a woman in today's world."
—**LIZA DONNELLY**, *New Yorker* cartoonist and writer, author of the history *Very Funny Ladies: The New Yorker's Women Cartoonists*

"Sarah is brilliant and reading her book is like being consoled by your funny, smart friend who just gets it on a deep level."
—**SAMANTHA ROTHENBERG** (Violet Clair), illustrator

WHY YOU'LL NEVER FIND THE ONE

And Why It Doesn't Matter

SARAH AKINTERINWA

PA PRESS

PRINCETON ARCHITECTURAL PRESS
NEW YORK

Contents

Preface

Hi, I'm Sarah Akinterinwa! I'm a cartoonist, illustrator, and writer. Being both a creative and a hopeless romantic has led me to a career in which I often get to draw and write about love, sex, relationships, and dating. I started my art career as a young millennial Black woman fresh out of a relationship and a job, in the middle of a pandemic, with nothing but a heavy heart and a small sliver of hope that I could make something of myself. But I knew that I had a lot to tell the world about what dating looks like for people like me. With a degree in humanistic counseling and my own complex (and borderline comical) dating experiences, I have always been fascinated by this subject, and I've picked up some valuable tools and wisdom that I now have the privilege of sharing in this book.

I know that all types of love, sex, relationships, and dating styles are unique to the individual, and I think it's important to note that the advice in this book comes from my own perspective as a cis-het woman. The spectrum of thoughts, feelings, and reactions that came out of my experiences have inspired the stories of the main character of this comic. That said, I hope that my work makes an impact on you no matter what walk of life you're from. I incorporated many versions of myself into this book, each of which helped me develop a perspective on love and relationships that I needed at the time. No matter your reason for picking up *Why You'll Never Find the One*, I hope it brings you comfort, insight, and laughter.

INTRODUCTION

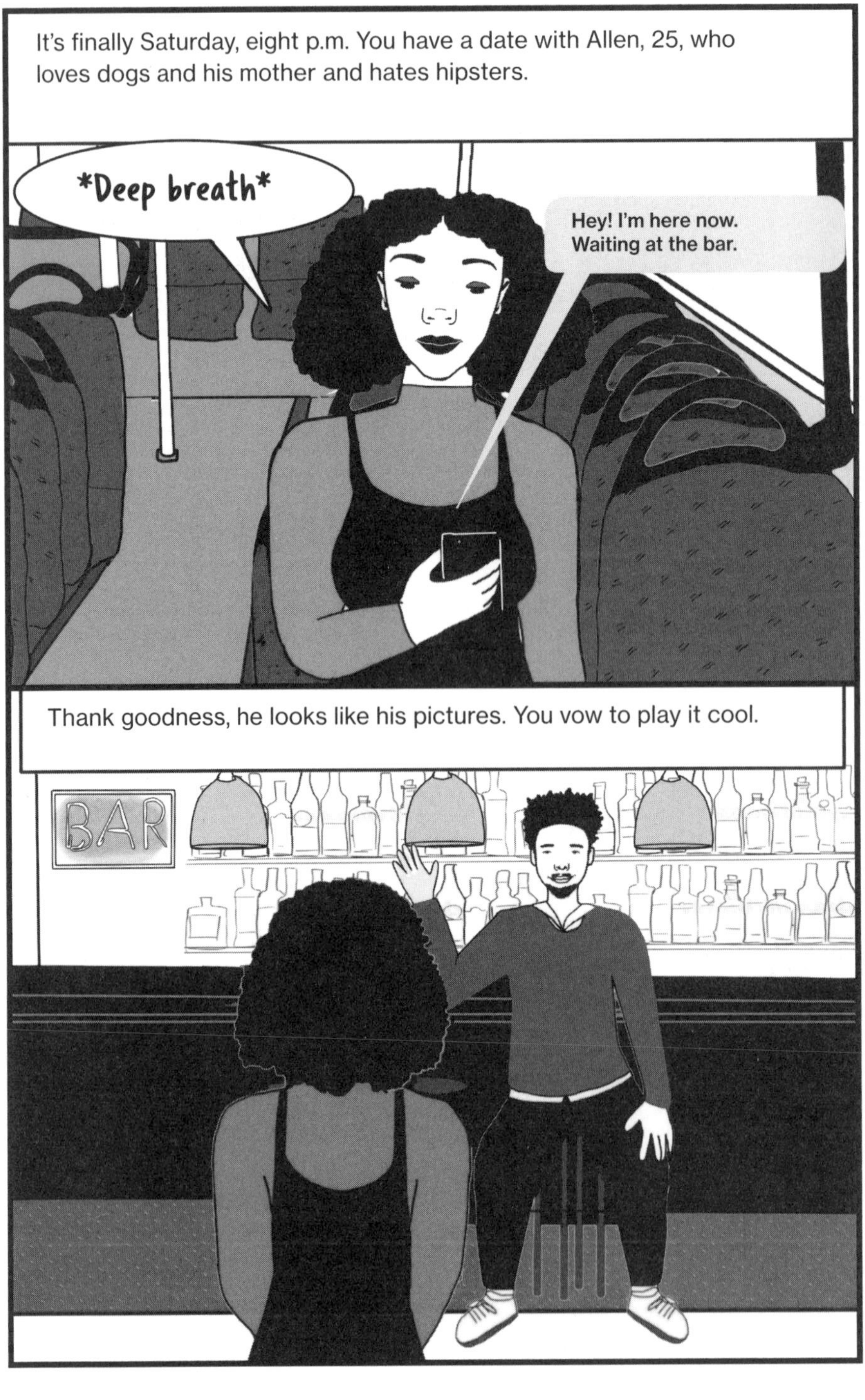
It's finally Saturday, eight p.m. You have a date with Allen, 25, who loves dogs and his mother and hates hipsters.
Deep breath
Hey! I'm here now. Waiting at the bar.
Thank goodness, he looks like his pictures. You vow to play it cool.
BAR

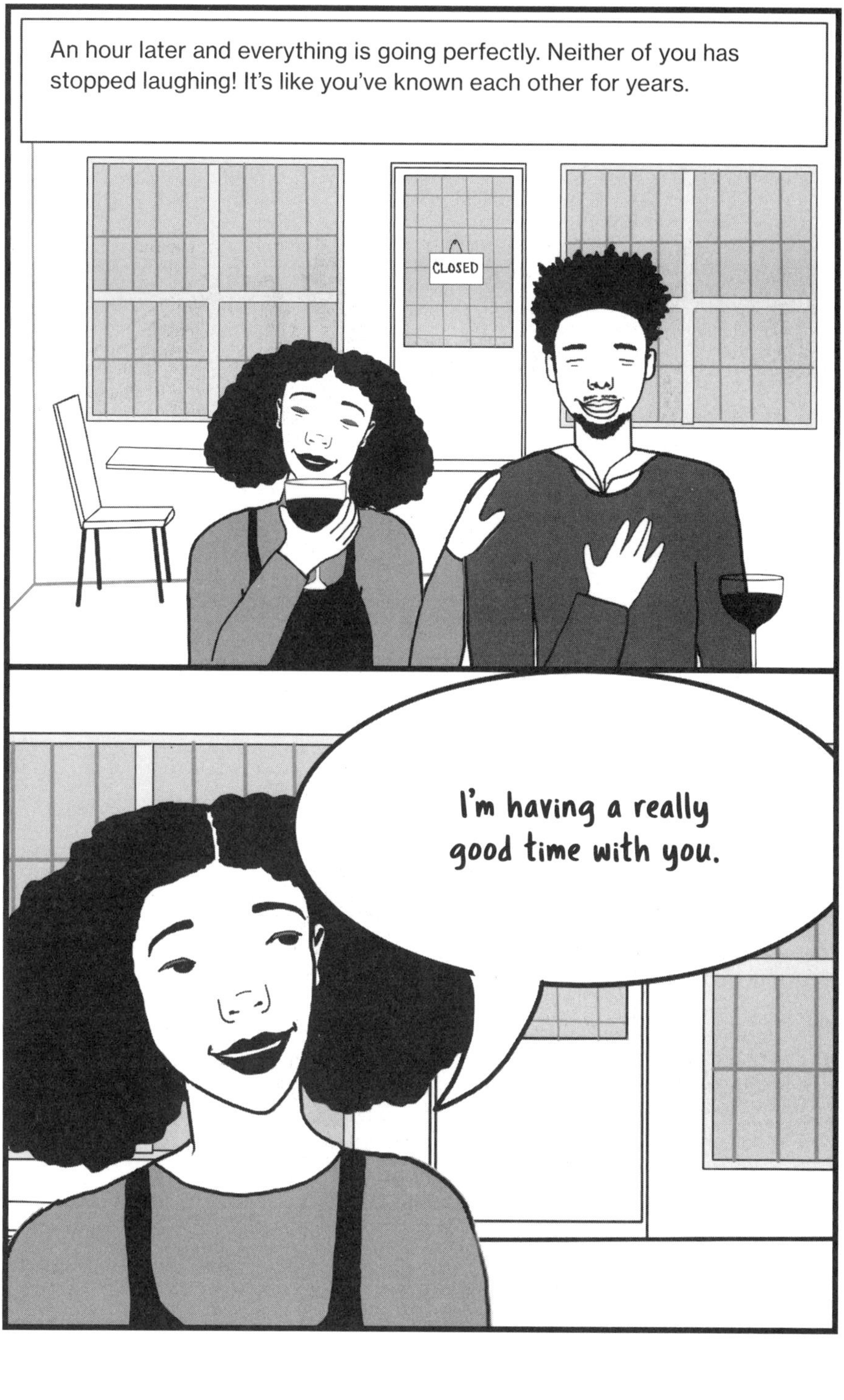
An hour later and everything is going perfectly. Neither of you has stopped laughing! It's like you've known each other for years.
CLOSED
I'm having a really good time with you.

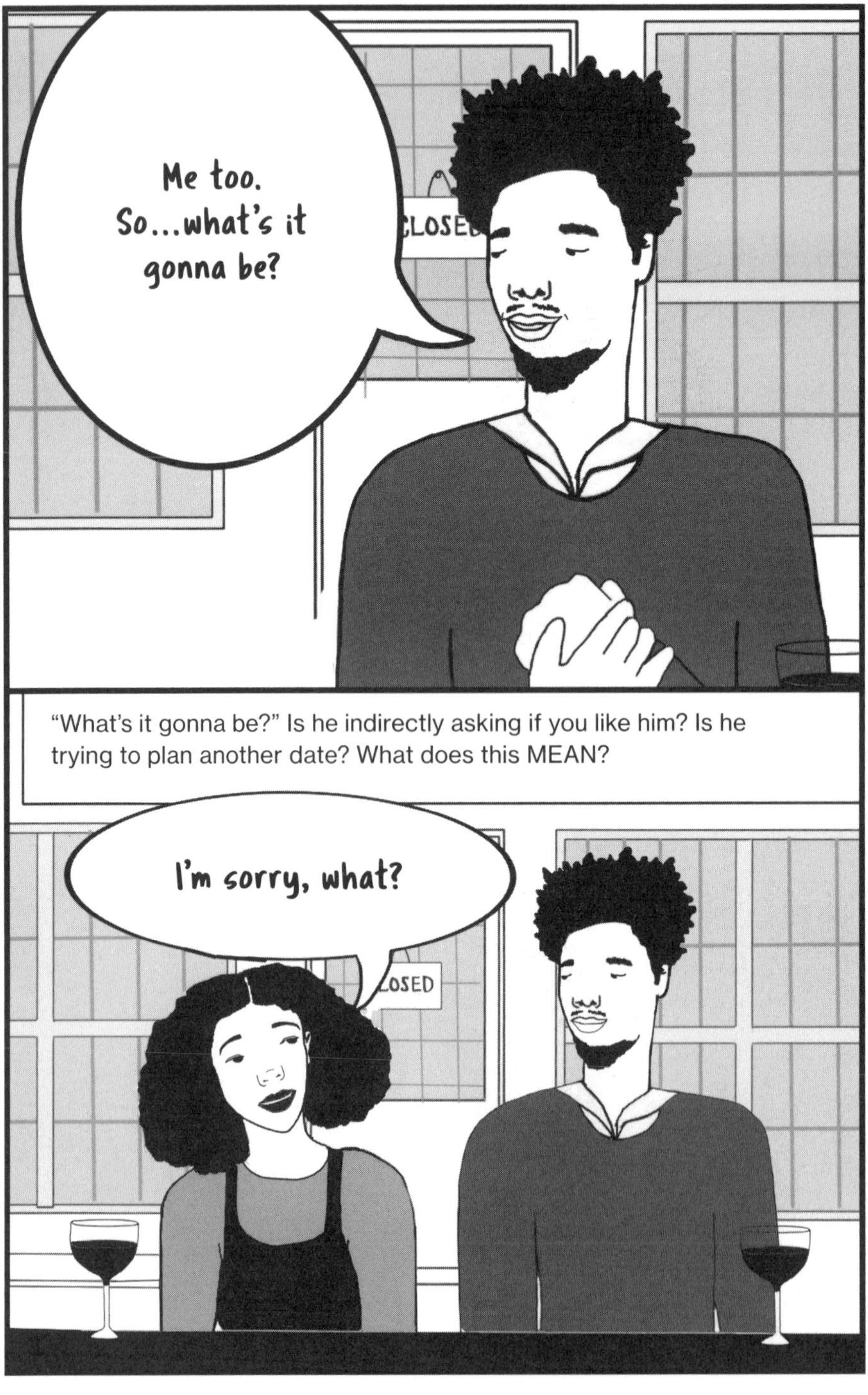
Me too. So...what's it gonna be?
"What's it gonna be?" Is he indirectly asking if you like him? Is he trying to plan another date? What does this MEAN?
I'm sorry, what?

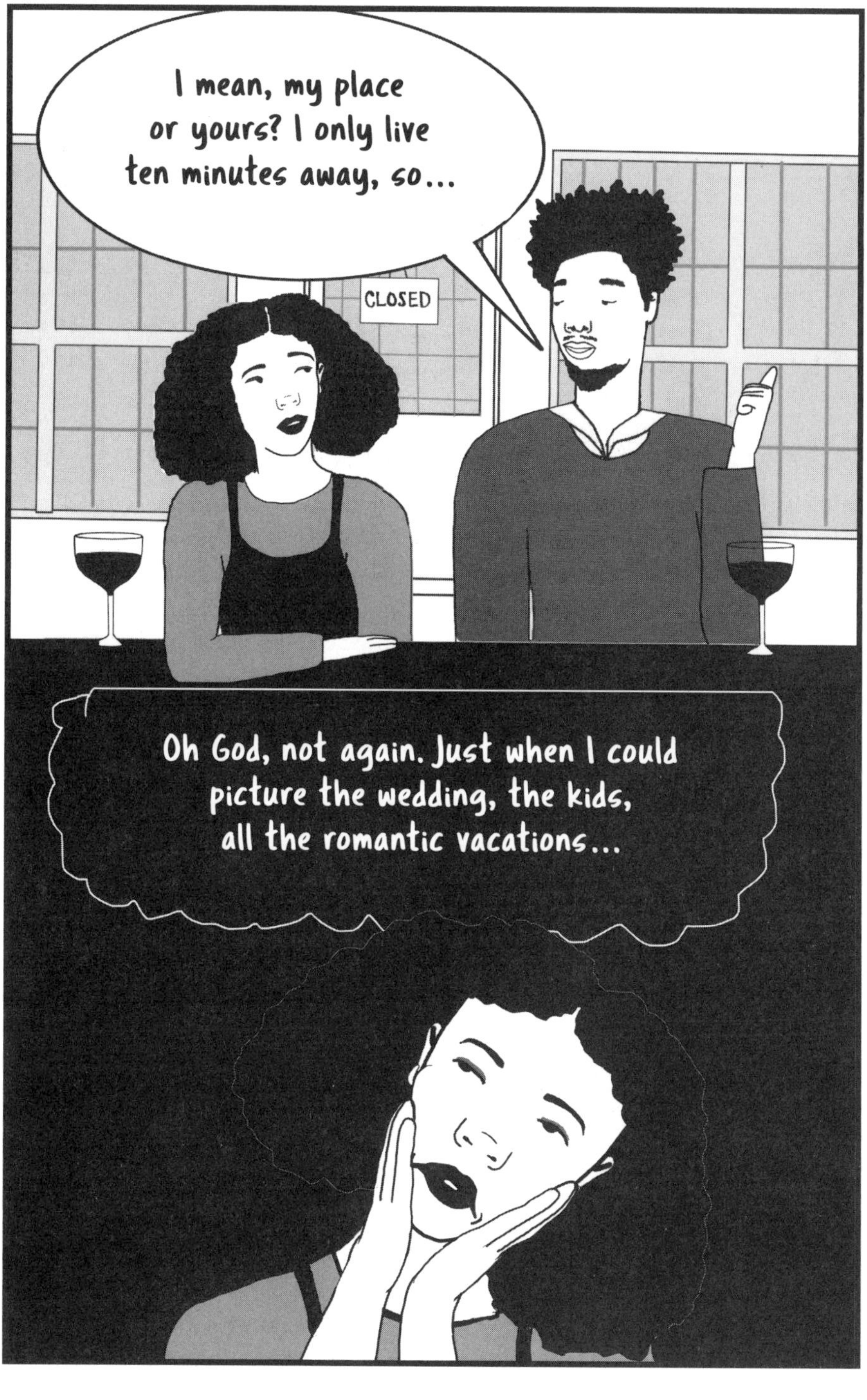
I mean, my place or yours? I only live ten minutes away, so...
CLOSED
Oh God, not again. Just when I could picture the wedding, the kids, all the romantic vacations...

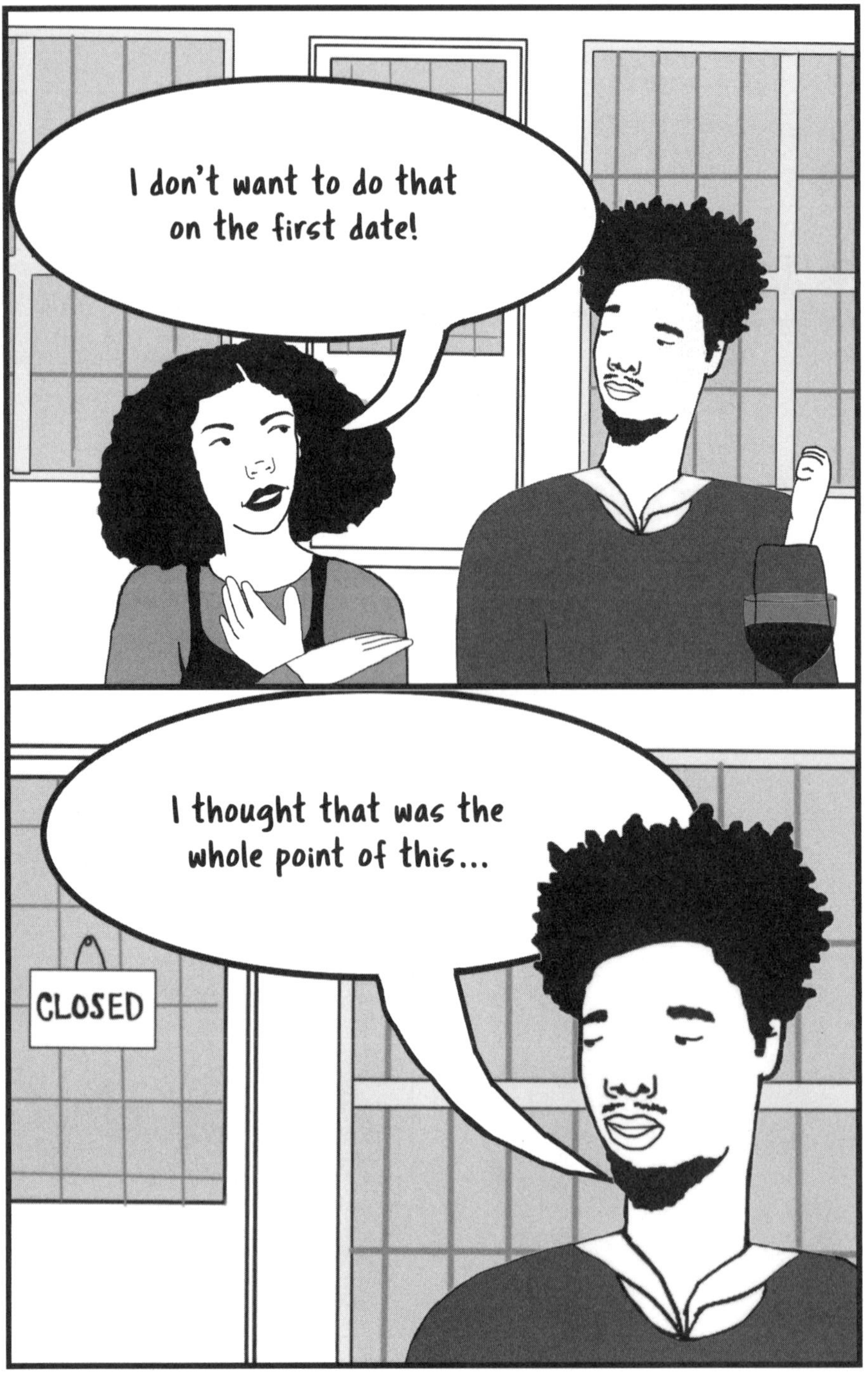
I don't want to do that on the first date!
I thought that was the whole point of this...
CLOSED

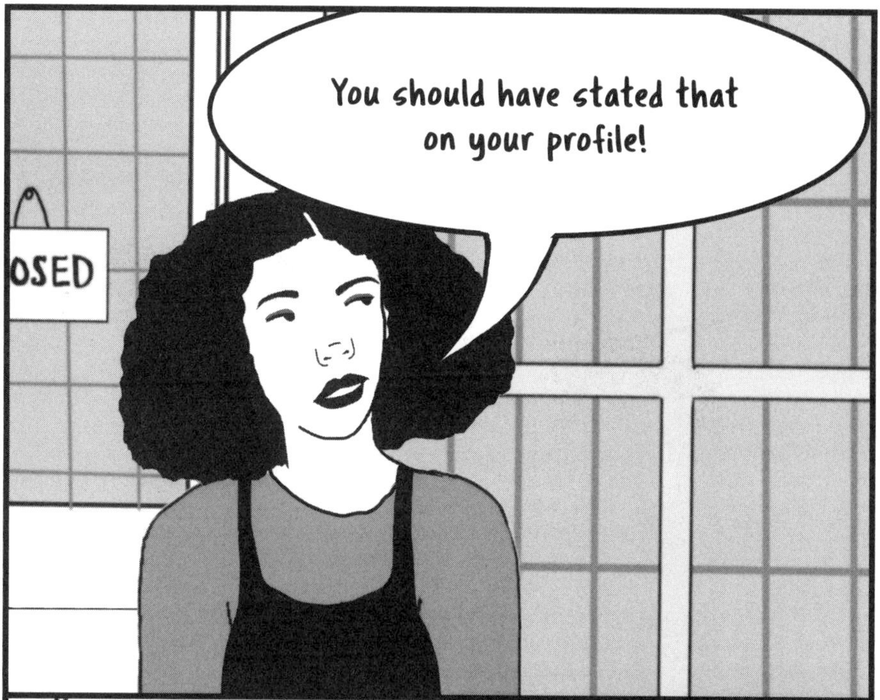
You should have stated that on your profile!
OSED

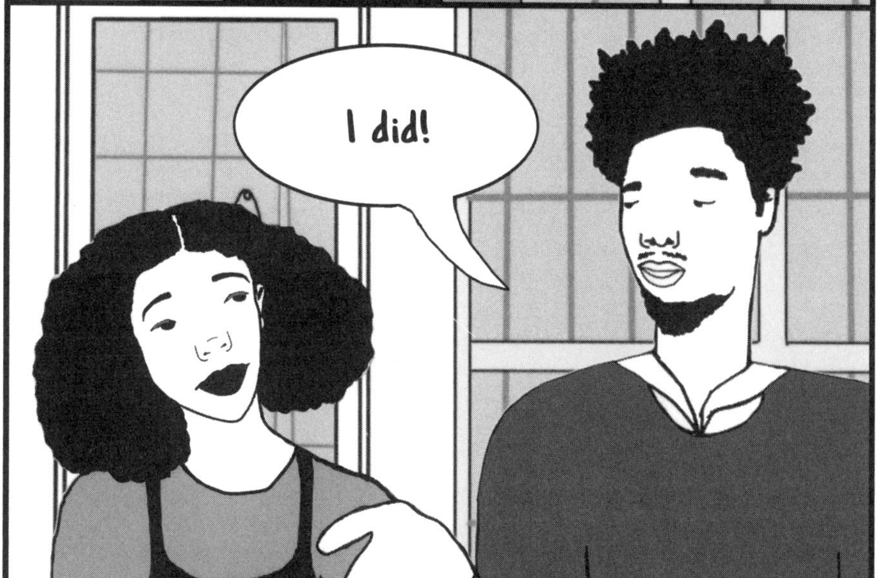
I did!

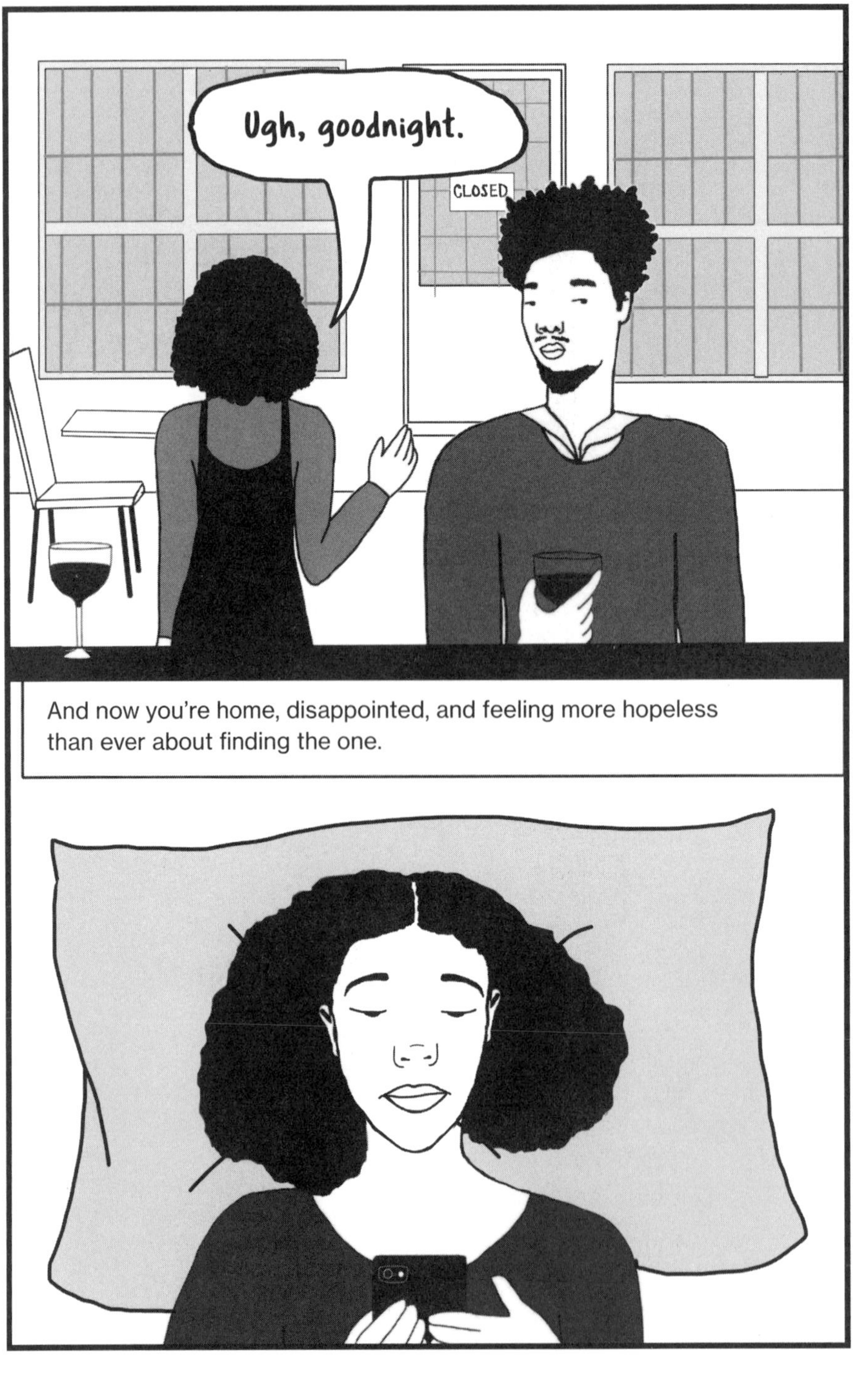
Ugh, goodnight.
CLOSED
And now you're home, disappointed, and feeling more hopeless than ever about finding the one.

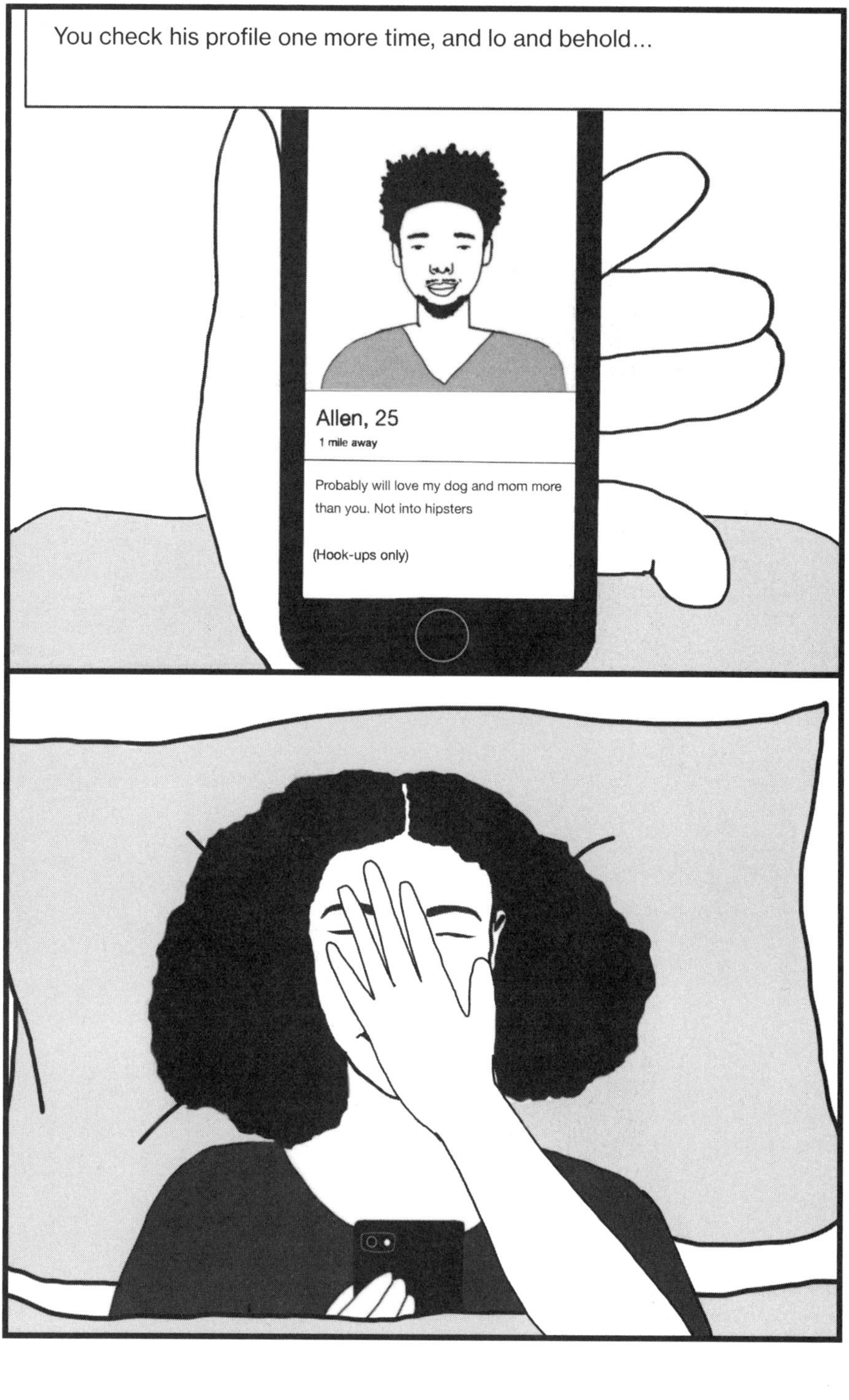
You check his profile one more time, and lo and behold...
Allen, 25
1 mile away
Probably will love my dog and mom more than you. Not into hipsters
(Hook-ups only)

CHAPTER ONE

WE ARE ALL VICTIMS OF ROMANTICIZATION

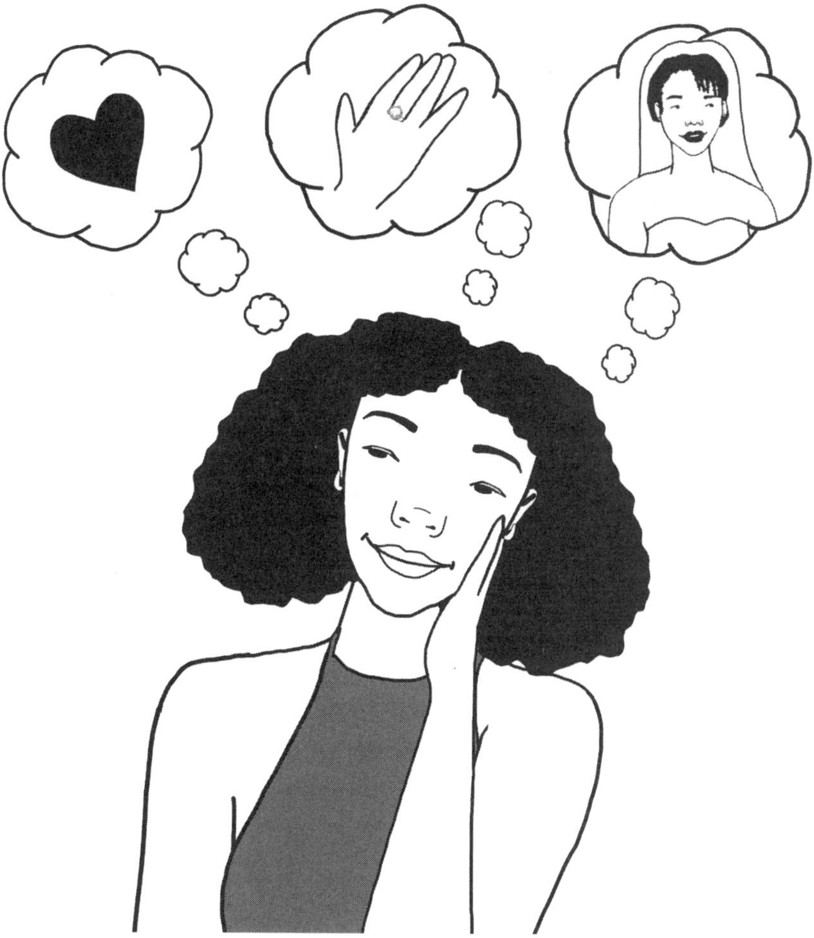

We Are All Victims of Romanticization

Raise your hand if you feel personally victimized by fairy tales, Disney movies, and rom-coms that push the urgent narrative of finding "the one." Now you're an adult, frustrated by your love life, and wondering why Prince Charming hasn't turned up at your door with your missing heel after a wild night out. While young adults today are in no rush to tie the knot, many of us are still very keen to experience a certain romanticized kind of relationship—and it's helpful to realize that it's not the only option available to us!

 Whatever generation you are in, it's likely you grew up on popular movies and TV shows in which couples are often two conventionally attractive people—and most often two cisgender, heterosexual white people. It's usually the same pattern: there's a buildup of tension between the primary characters, but they're somehow kept apart by various factors such as busy jobs, an existing marriage, or the fear that a romance would ruin a good friendship. The idea is to convince us viewers that these two people are "soul mates." But how many times have you witnessed a fictional couple whose relationship couldn't possibly work due to blindingly obvious incompatibilities? Maybe at a certain point, you started to think it might not be the end of the world if they moved on and dated other people. There are so many other ways to think about dating and finding love.

Family systems also play a role in shaping idealized images of love. The earliest examples of love we are exposed to—that of our parents, grandparents, and other caregivers and adults in our childhood—teach us what to expect from our own love lives. For instance, if your parents consciously treat each other respectfully, communicate effectively during disagreements, and display romantic love in a healthy, nurturing way, they are demonstrating a positive approach to relationships that you will have learned how to replicate in your own life. In contrast, if your parents regularly display signs of incompatibility, visualizing yourself in a healthy committed relationship may not come easily.

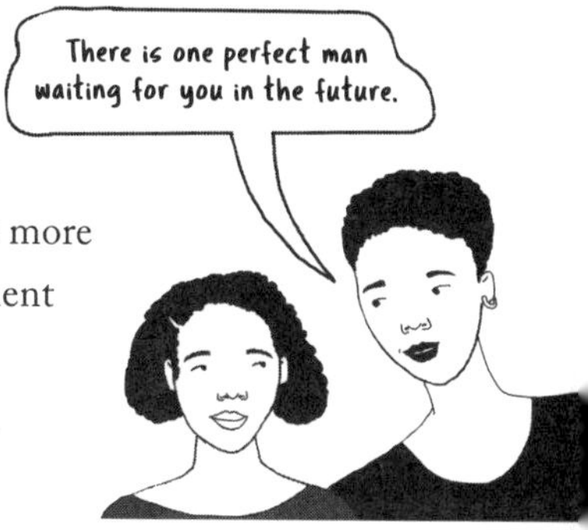
There is one perfect man waiting for you in the future.

Consider what kinds of ideas about relationships you might have if your parents have struggled to get along. Multiple studies show that the children of couples who don't have healthy relationships are more likely to have insecure attachment styles, commitment issues, and marriages that end in divorce. In short, it's not your fault if your love life is grim—you can blame your parents for that. The good news is that there are many useful tools to access, from therapy to podcasts and books by relationship experts and even YouTube channels and other social media pages dedicated to dating and relationship advice. We can use these tools to develop self-awareness, understand our core beliefs about love, and seek out the relationships that truly work best for us.

Despite being part of a generation that fought for the equality of women in the workforce and in intimate relationships, our parents may also have passed on beliefs about relationships that can discourage our pursuing partnerships that reflect our true selves—such as the belief that romance should only exist between cisgender, heterosexual (or "cis-het") men and women, that women must wait for love to come to them rather than pursue it herself, or that a woman is only truly independent if she doesn't get married. Isn't it awesome that we now live in a time when such restrictive beliefs are being dismissed and more people are starting to realize that love looks different to everyone across the spectrum of gender and sexuality? Nonetheless, we can't deny the effects these long-held beliefs have on our outlooks on love.

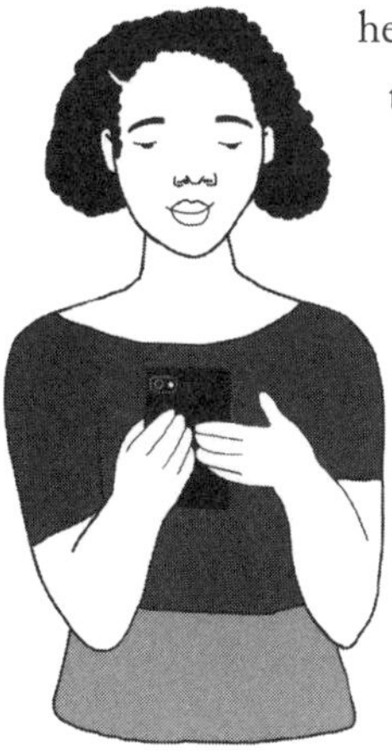

And then there's social media. For members of the first generation to grow up with social media—a space where influencers, celebrities, and even our own family and friends share all the best parts of their relationships (leaving out the mundane and difficult moments)—it's no wonder they have developed unattainable fantasies about IRL romance.

Despite it sometimes feeling like we are living in a lovelorn era, there is an abundance of dating resources: TV shows about dating, dating how-to guides, and dating apps. In some ways dating—whomever and however one chooses—is more accessible now than ever. We are "Generation Tinder," with thousands of profiles of prospective partners always at our disposal. So why is it so hard to actually *date* someone?

Imagine if we could take control of our love lives and go after what we want without the hang-ups and limitations that come with the prescribed gender roles and ideas of how love stories should unfold that are so foundational to contemporary dating culture. Believe it or not, it's possible! Dating in this millennium starts with deconstructing your ideas about love, getting to know your positive qualities and your flaws, and accepting that off-screen relationships require compatibility and self-awareness to thrive. *And* recognizing that feeling loved, desirable, and worthy isn't exclusive to romantic partnerships. We also have to learn how to make the first move and get cozy with the reality of disappointment and rejection. Oh, and enjoy being single while we're at it!

Nothing too difficult, right?

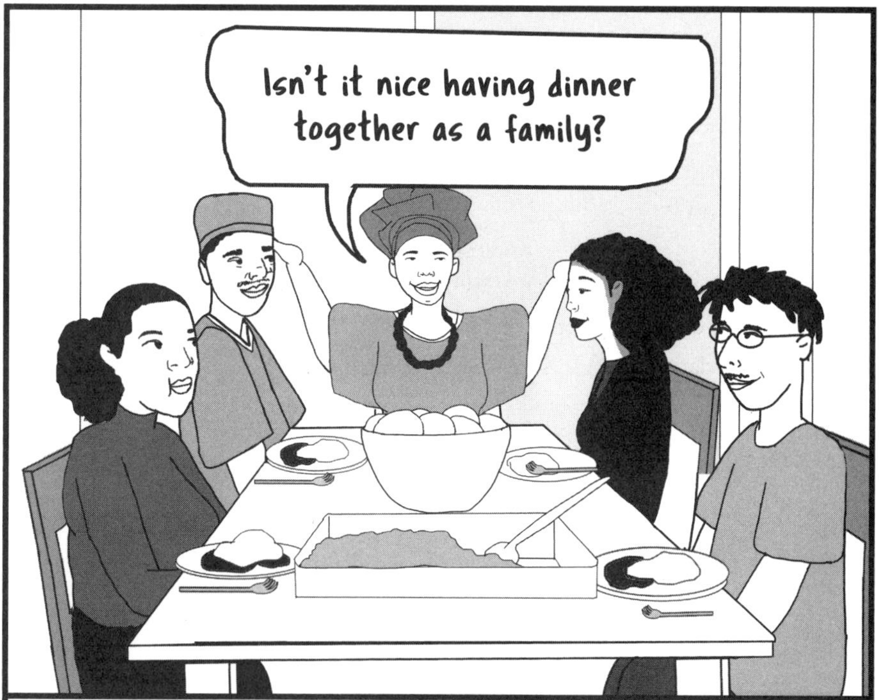
Isn't it nice having dinner together as a family?

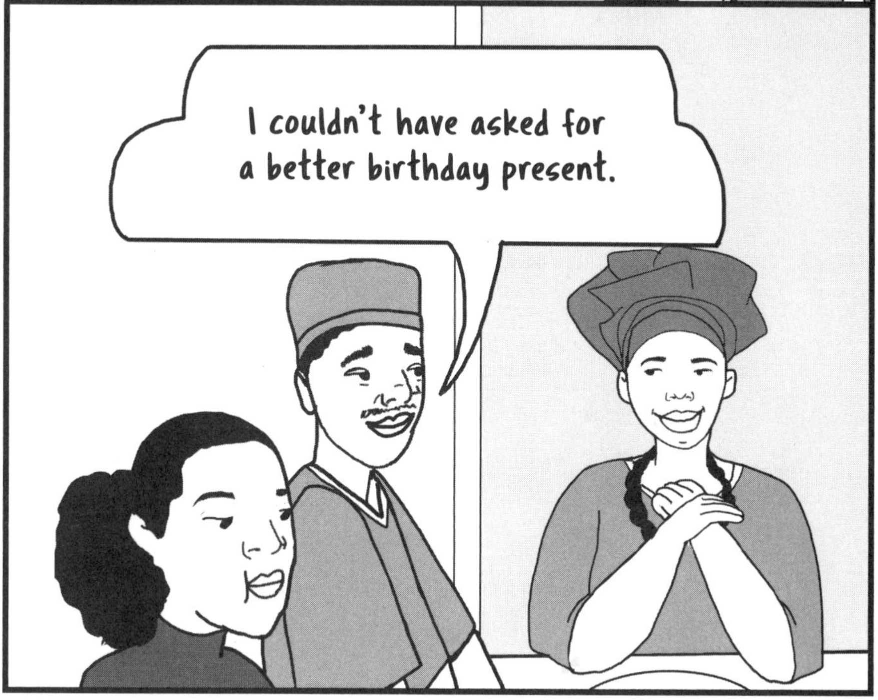
I couldn't have asked for a better birthday present.

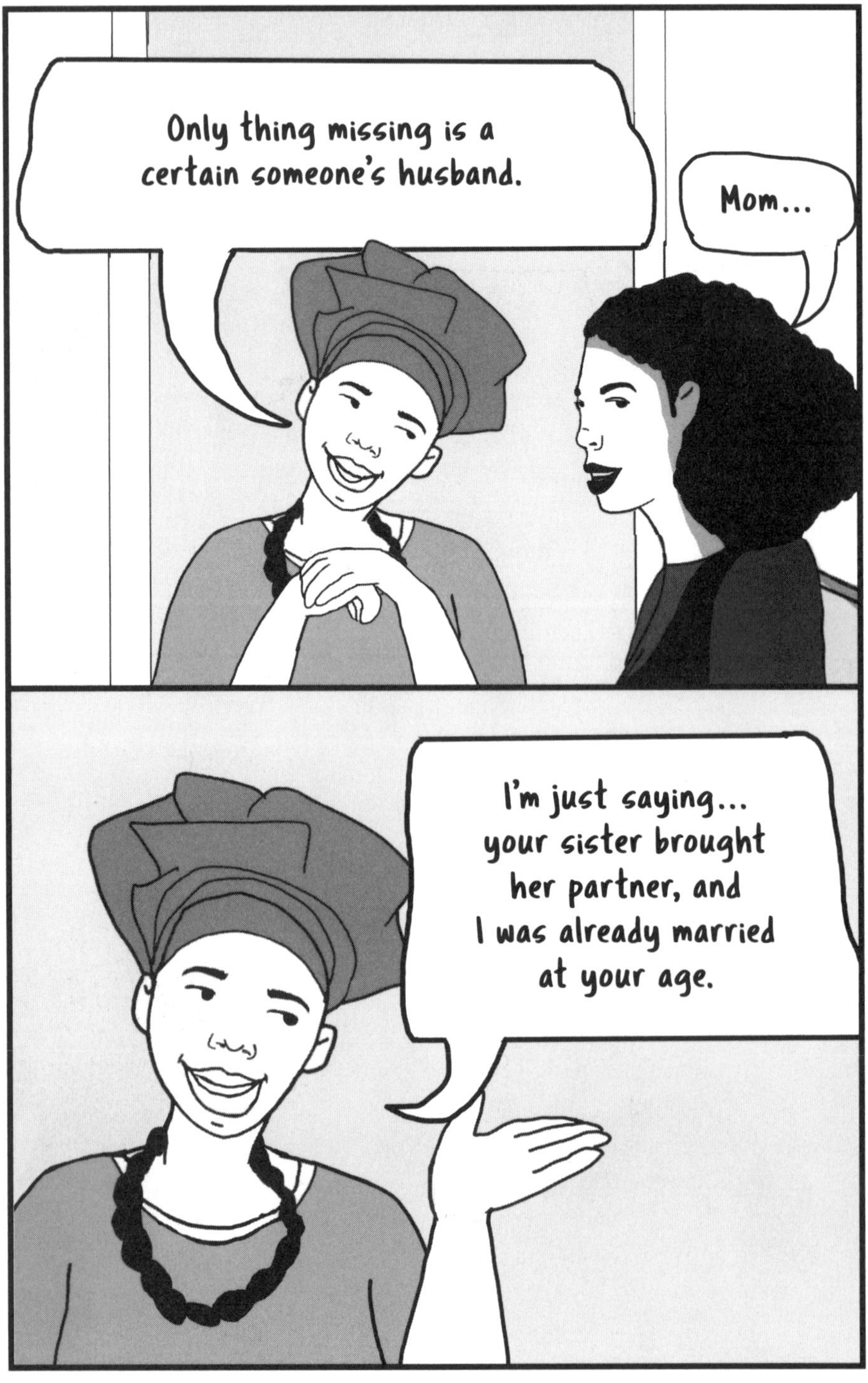
Only thing missing is a certain someone's husband.
Mom...
I'm just saying... your sister brought her partner, and I was already married at your age.

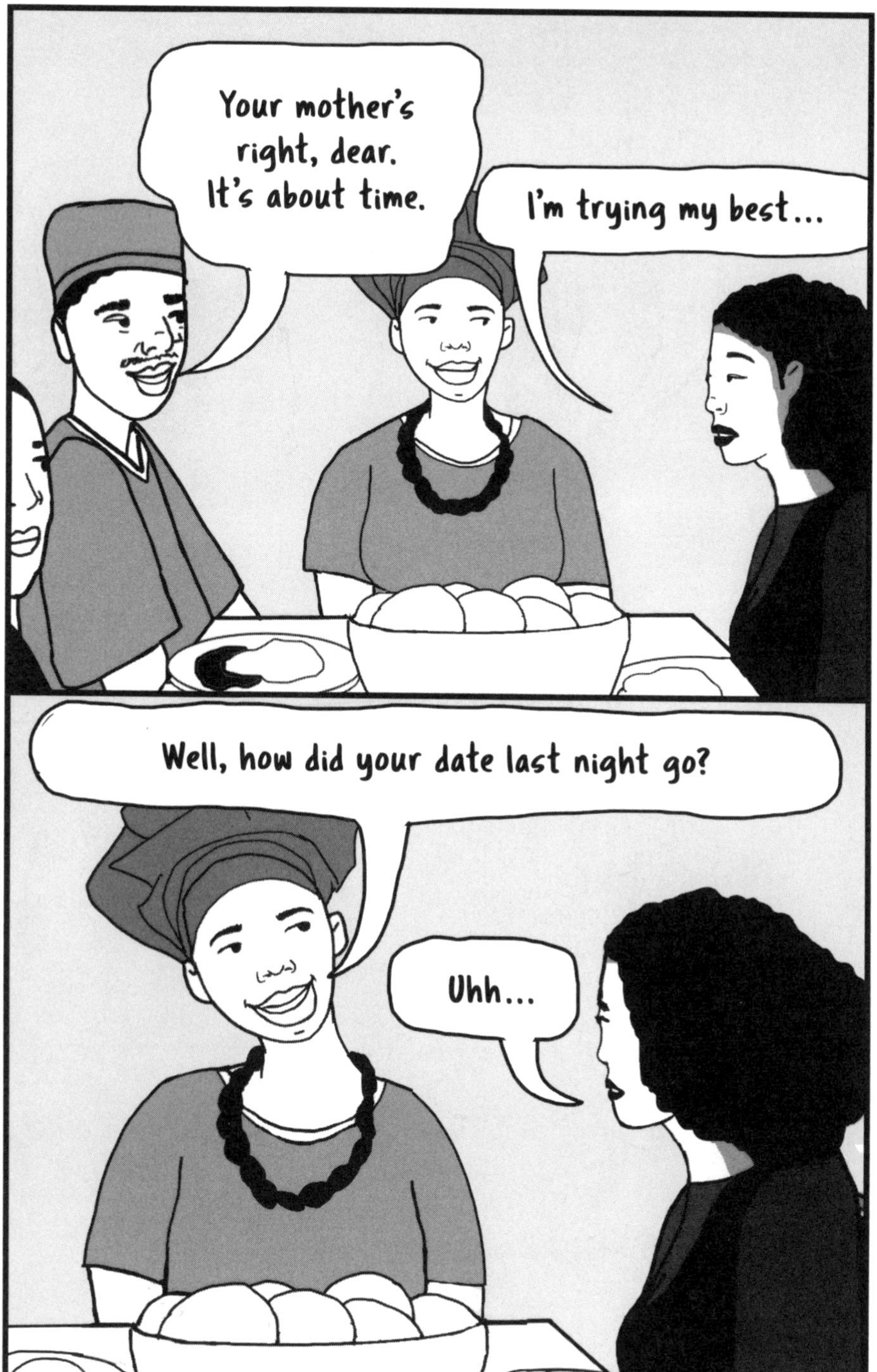
Your mother's right, dear. It's about time.
I'm trying my best...
Well, how did your date last night go?
Uhh...

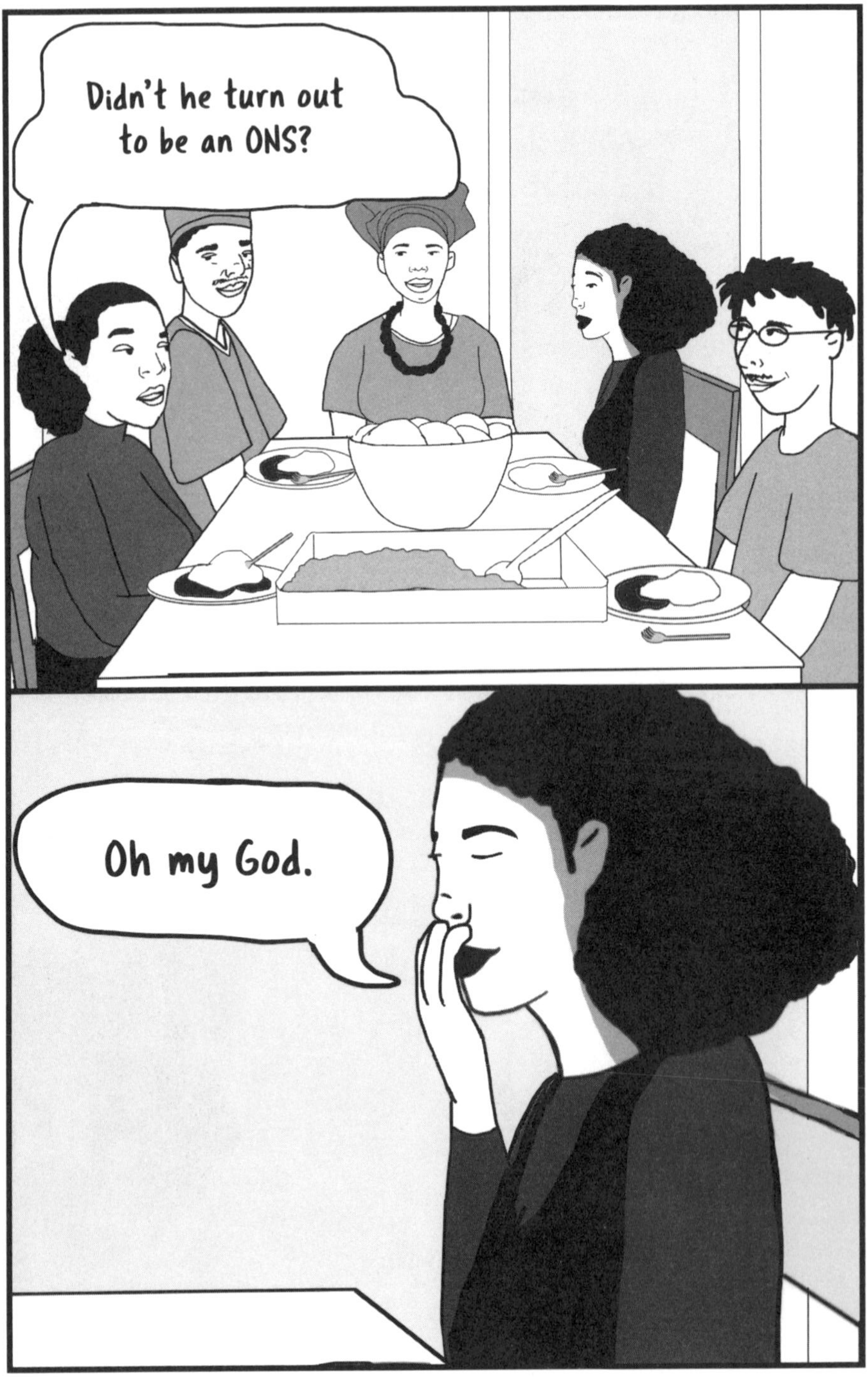
Didn't he turn out to be an ONS?
Oh my God.

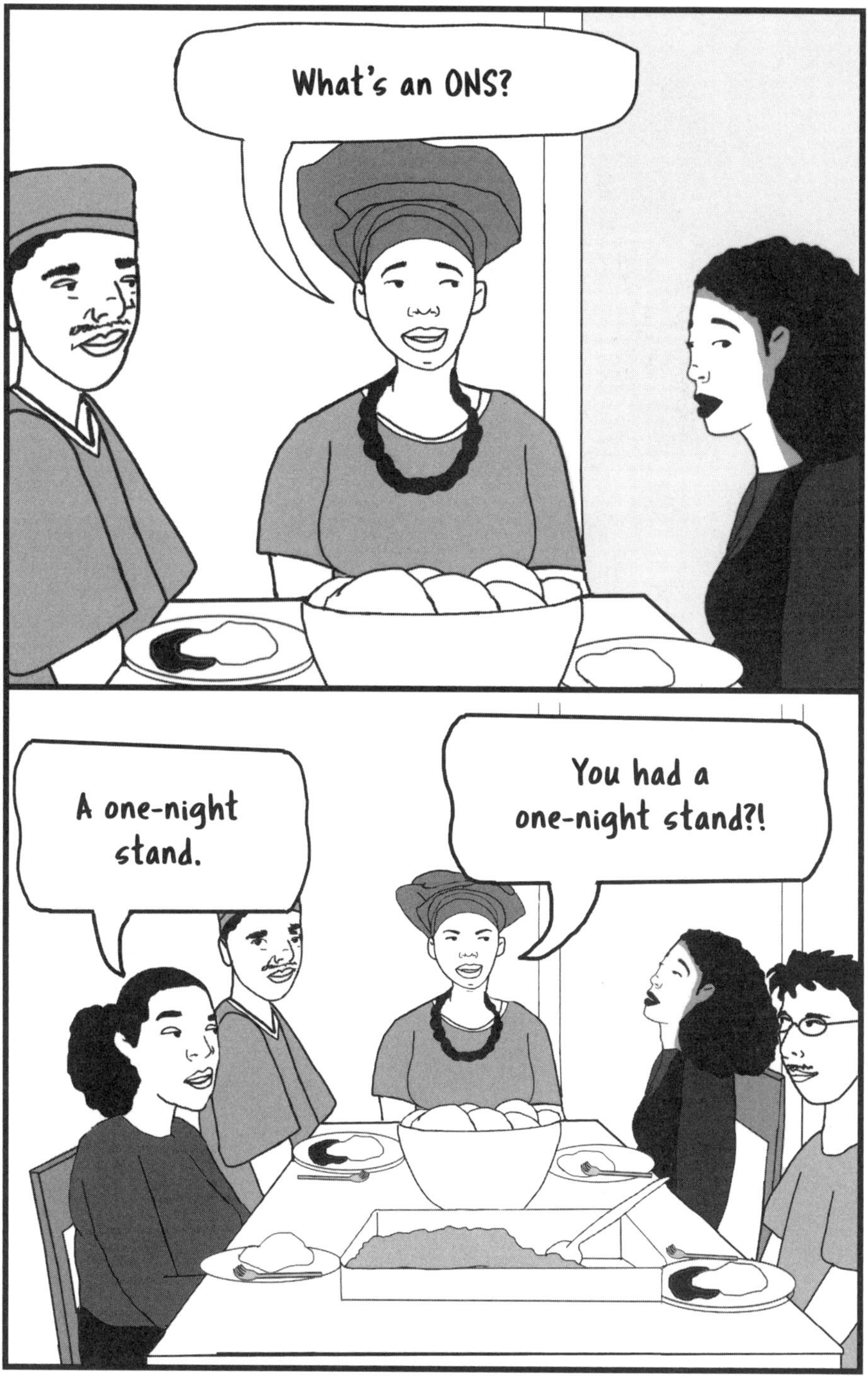
What's an ONS?
A one-night stand.
You had a one-night stand?!

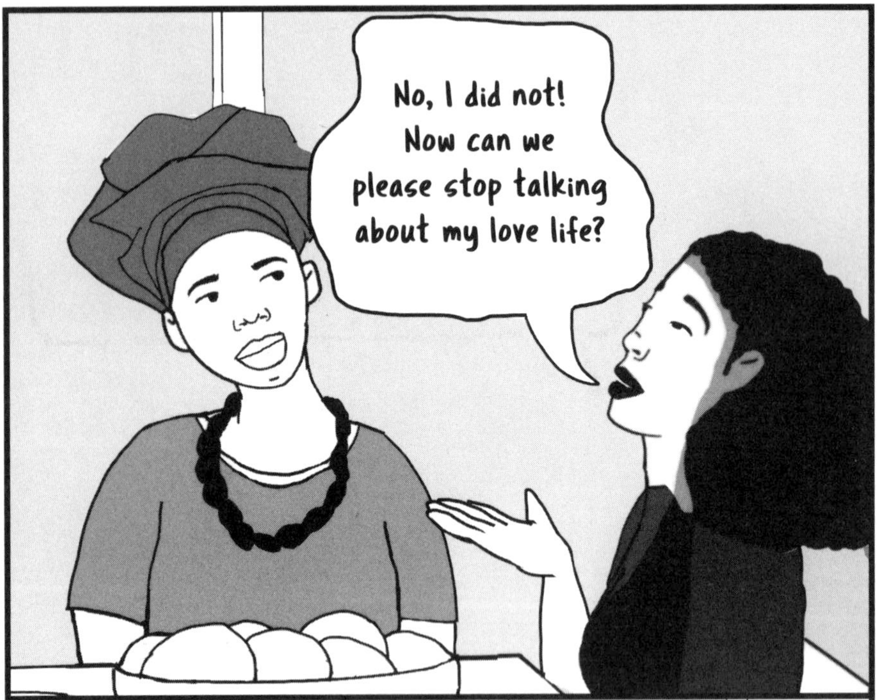
No, I did not! Now can we please stop talking about my love life?

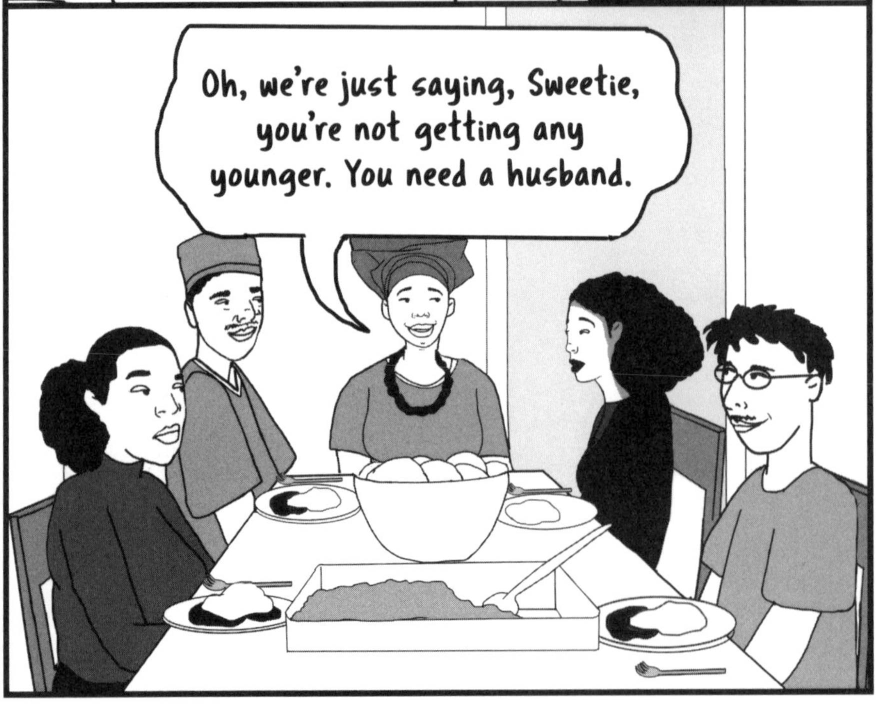
Oh, we're just saying, Sweetie, you're not getting any younger. You need a husband.

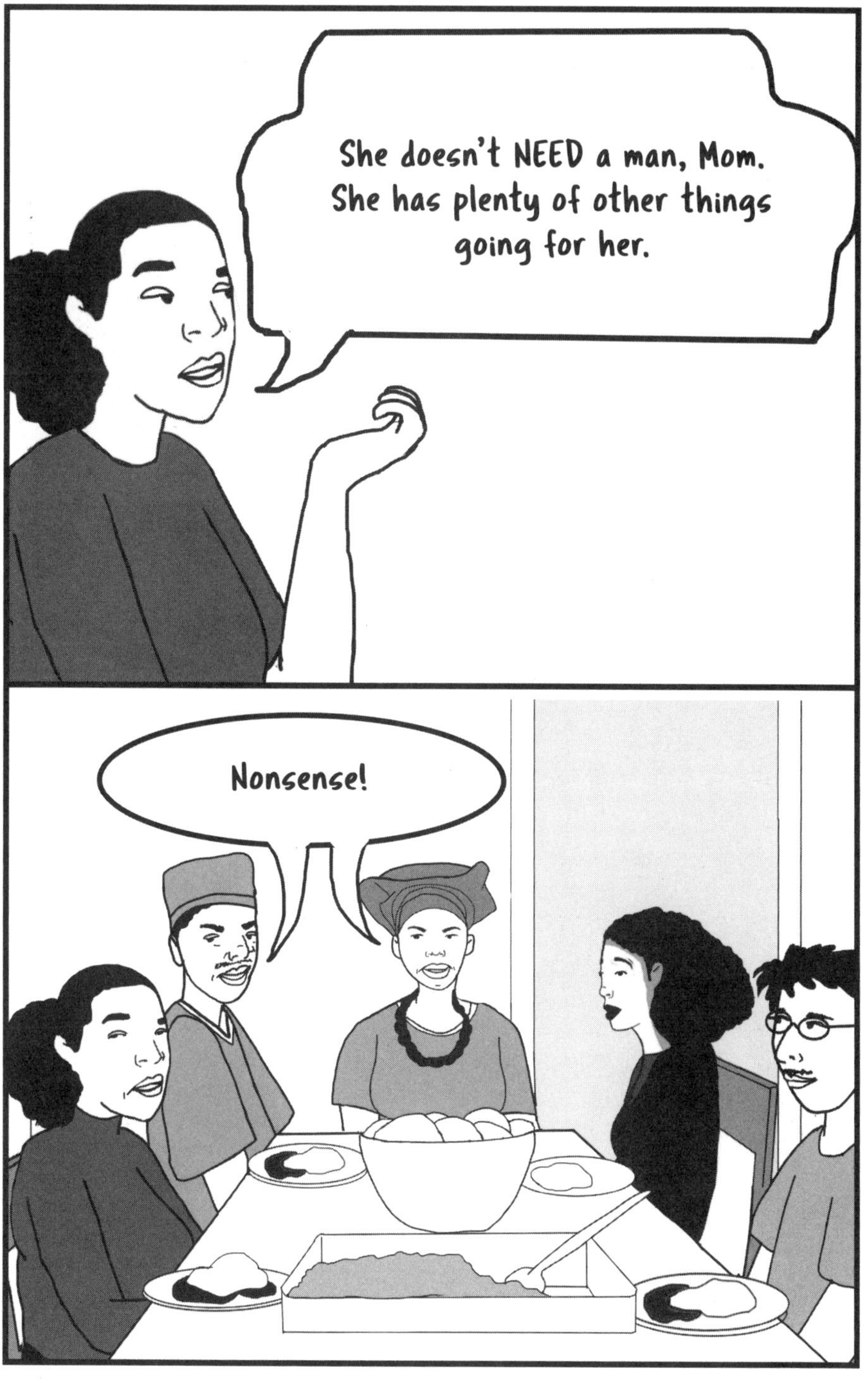
She doesn't NEED a man, Mom. She has plenty of other things going for her.
Nonsense!

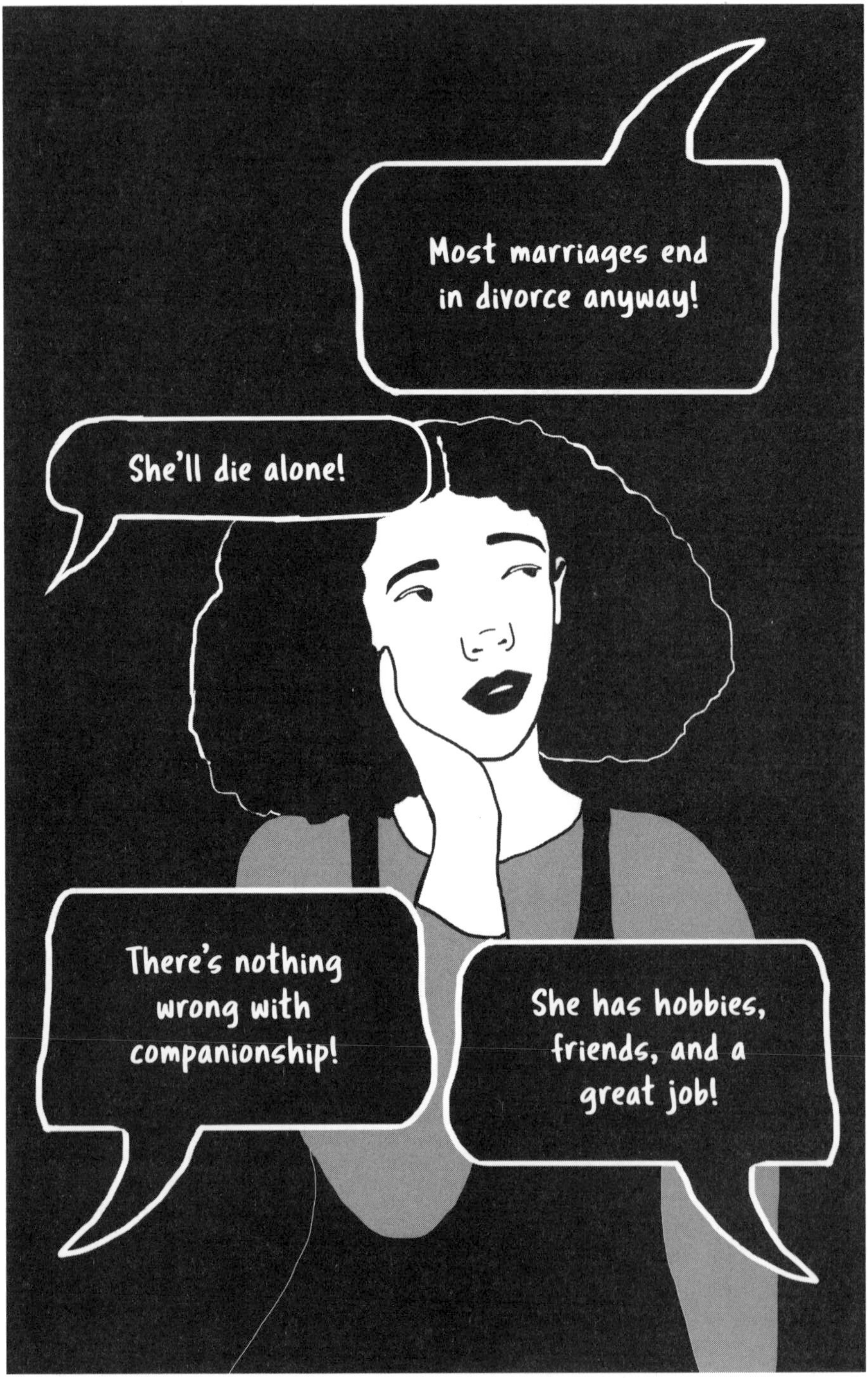
Most marriages end in divorce anyway!
She'll die alone!
There's nothing wrong with companionship!
She has hobbies, friends, and a great job!

—

No one
is allowed to
pressure
you to stay
single or
pursue love.

—

CHAPTER TWO

DOES THE PERSON YOU WANT EVEN EXIST?

Does the Person You Want Even Exist?

Wanting a relationship is simple, but figuring out what you *actually* want from a relationship is more complex. Do you want a person to call your partner, or are there qualities and experiences you're seeking in a person that could enhance your life? The first step to feeling in control of your love life is to be clear about what kind of person you want to be with. You might already have a rough idea of what you're looking for: How does this person compare to the people you've dated in the past? How much do they reflect your current stage of personal development? For instance, do you want someone who is open to marriage in the future? Are you avoiding a person with poor communication skills, like your last partner?

It's time to get specific. If you're to find someone you're compatible with, you'll need to consider what traits would best complement your own. It's okay to want someone who's nice and has a good job and a great sense of humor, but let's face it—many people have these qualities. Plus, they may be nice to *you*, but are they nice to the waiter who accidently spills a drink on their new shirt? They may be funny, but are their jokes at the expense of marginalized groups? They may have a good job, but is it a job they loathe and complain about whenever they get the chance?

Relationships expert Shan Boodram suggests approaching scouting for a partner as though it were a job search. This allows you to be specific and clear about what qualities make up the right candidate for you and gives fewer opportunities to the wrong ones so that you don't waste your time. According to Boodram, a clear "job listing" should be separated into a basic description of what you are looking for, areas of flexibility, and do-not-applies.

Your job listing might factor in things like location—do you want to be involved with someone who lives nearby, or are you indifferent to distance? You might also establish an acceptable age range—do you only want to

Mr. Meh

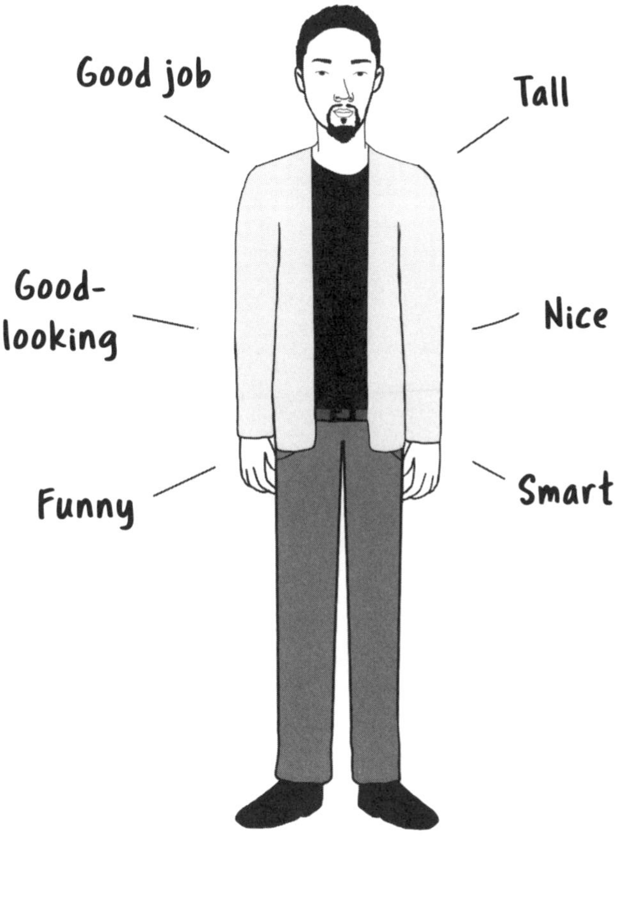
Good job
Tall
Good-
looking
Nice
Funny
Smart

partner with someone around your age, or does a greater age difference not matter? Most importantly, consider the basic requirements you seek in a partner that you're not willing to compromise on. For example, you might want to date someone who shares your political views, who is interested in having children one day, or who is open to being nonmonogamous.

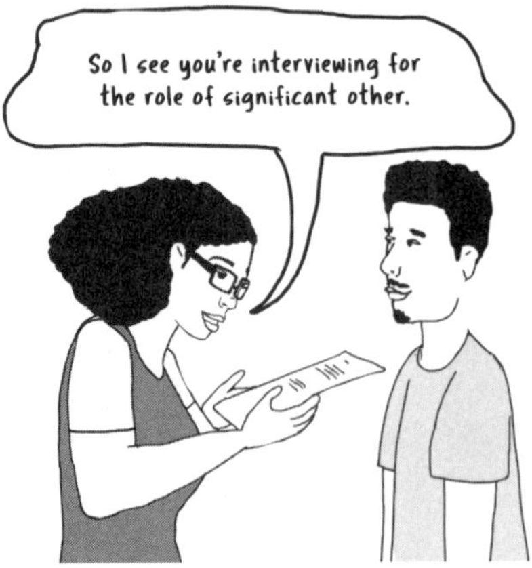
So I see you're interviewing for the role of significant other.

Once you've decided on your basic job listing, you can consider your areas of flexibility. This simply means factors that you can be flexible about because they're not as important to you as your nonnegotiables; for example, smoking, taste in music, race, or annual income. Finally, think about your do-not-applies. This means traits you are unwilling to tolerate in a partner, such as a short temper or poor personal hygiene. Once you've listed all these things, voilà—you have a job description and a clearer idea of what you're looking for.

I know what you're thinking: Where does physical attraction come in?

There's no denying that a person's appearance is one of the first things you notice and a big part of what attracts you to them. However, what if the person you connect with doesn't quite fit your type? While it's important to feel attracted to your partner, the truth is, physical appearance reveals very little about compatibility. After the initial butterflies settle down, anyone who is looking for something that goes beyond a purely physical relationship will be interested in getting to know a person's character. By fixating on a specific

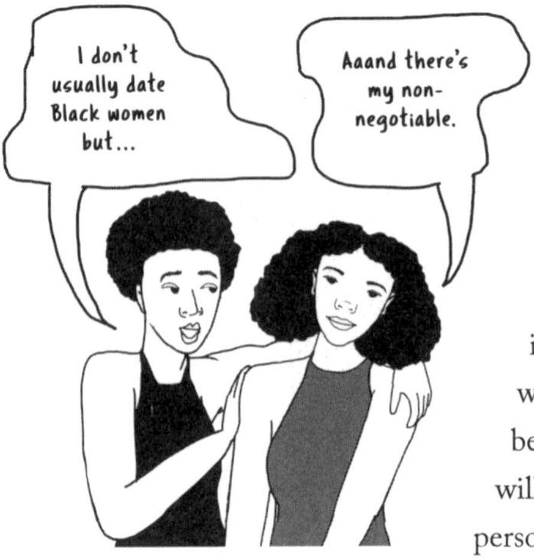
I don't usually date Black women but...
Aaand there's my non-negotiable.

set of physical traits, you may be significantly limiting your dating pool and missing out on opportunities to connect with the beautiful diversity of people you're compatible with.

Level of dating standards
Adolescence
20s
30s

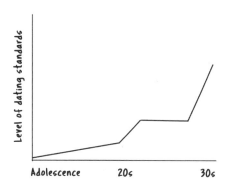

Remember, your life is happening right now in this moment! There's no need to remain attached to the vision you've always had of a perfect partner, especially if you've grown in ways that enable you to be open to something different. Honor your needs and standards by regularly revisiting your job listing and prioritizing qualities that are relevant to you and where you are in your life now. You can't have relationships with idealized, fantasy versions of people, but you can have them with real, raw human beings just like you.

How is it possible that both these people are my type?

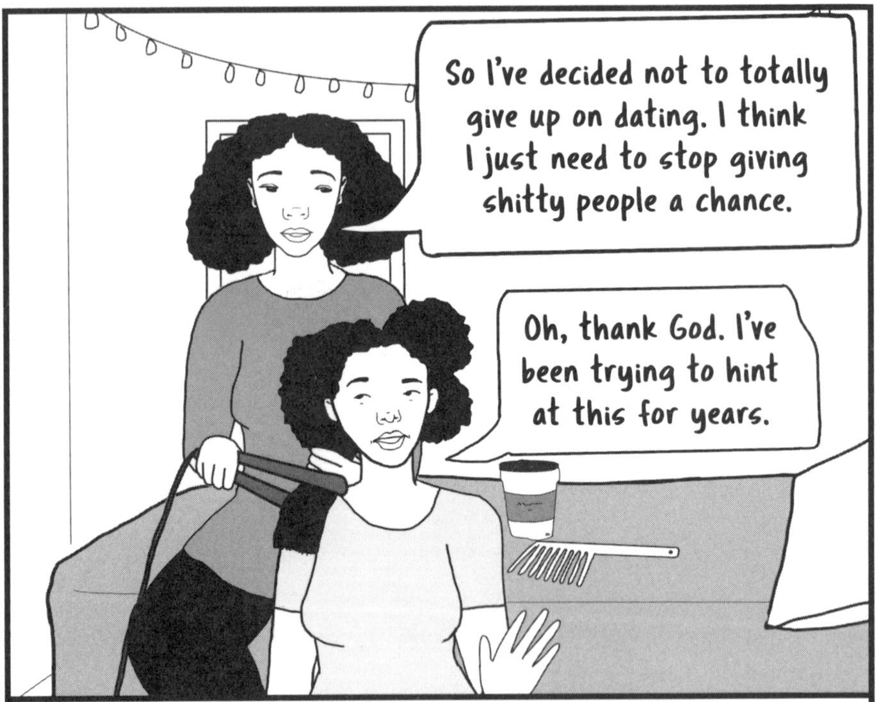
So I've decided not to totally give up on dating. I think I just need to stop giving shitty people a chance.
Oh, thank God. I've been trying to hint at this for years.

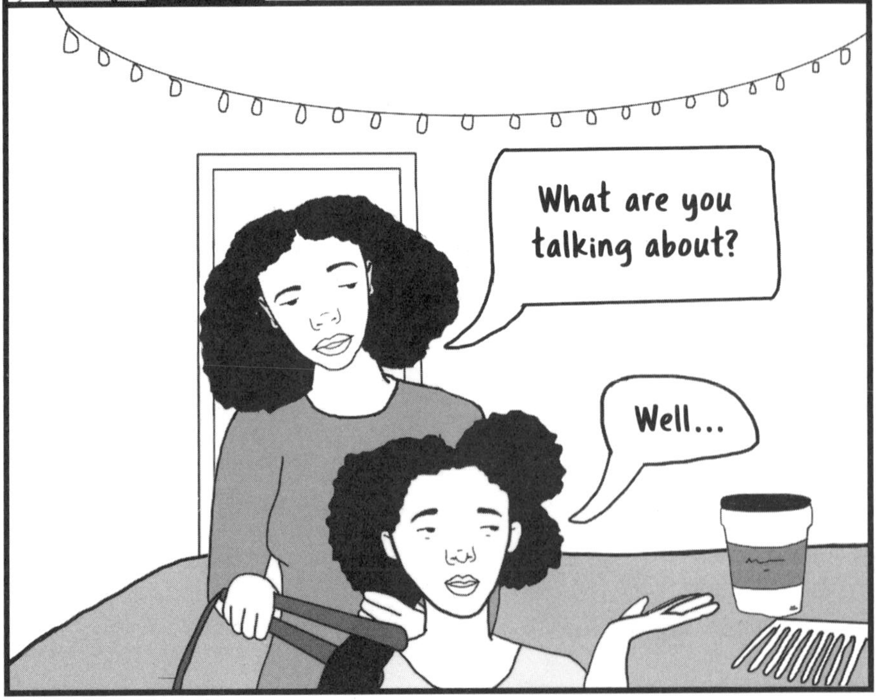
What are you talking about?
Well...

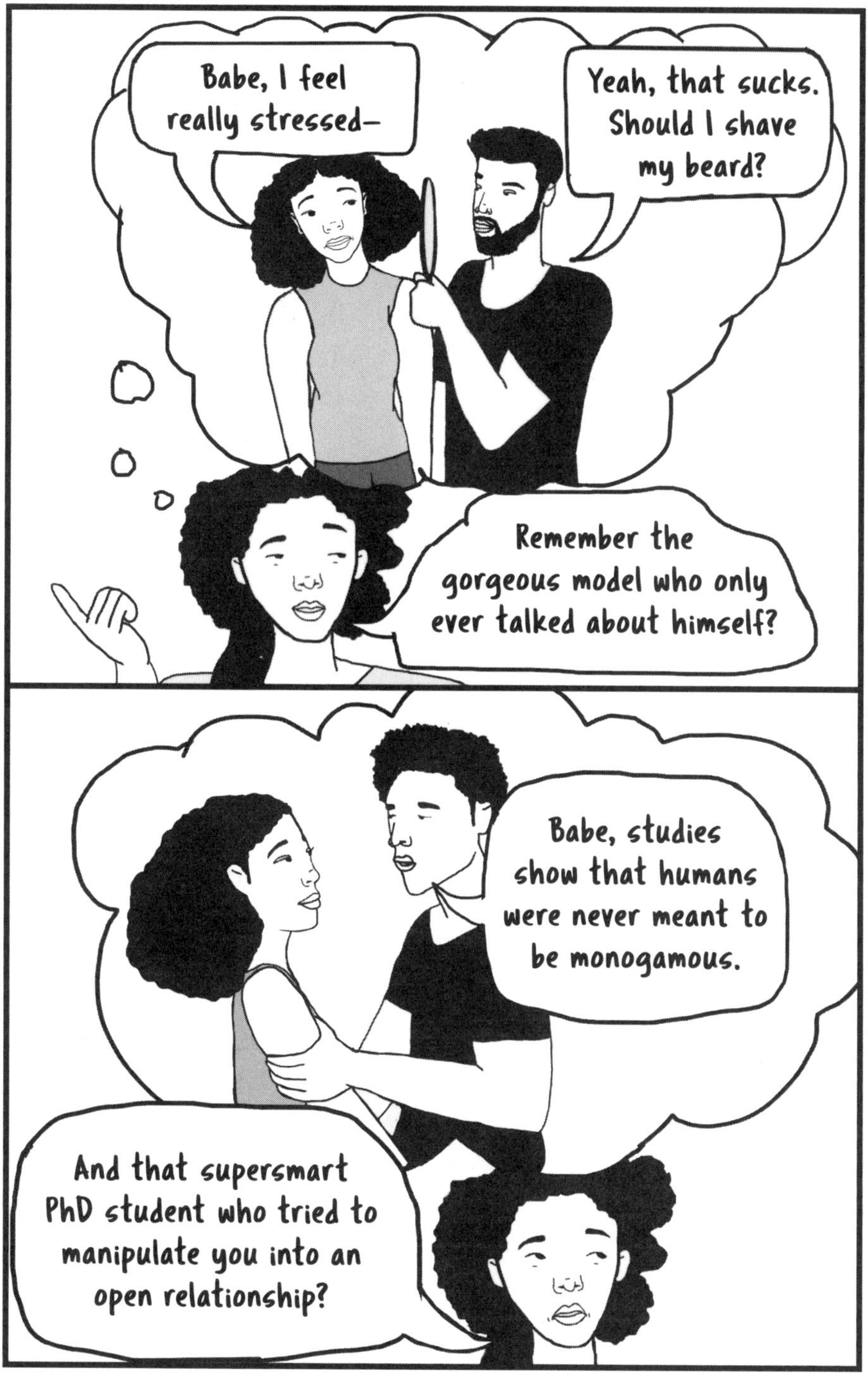
Babe, I feel really stressed—
Yeah, that sucks. Should I shave my beard?
Remember the gorgeous model who only ever talked about himself?
Babe, studies show that humans were never meant to be monogamous.
And that supersmart PhD student who tried to manipulate you into an open relationship?

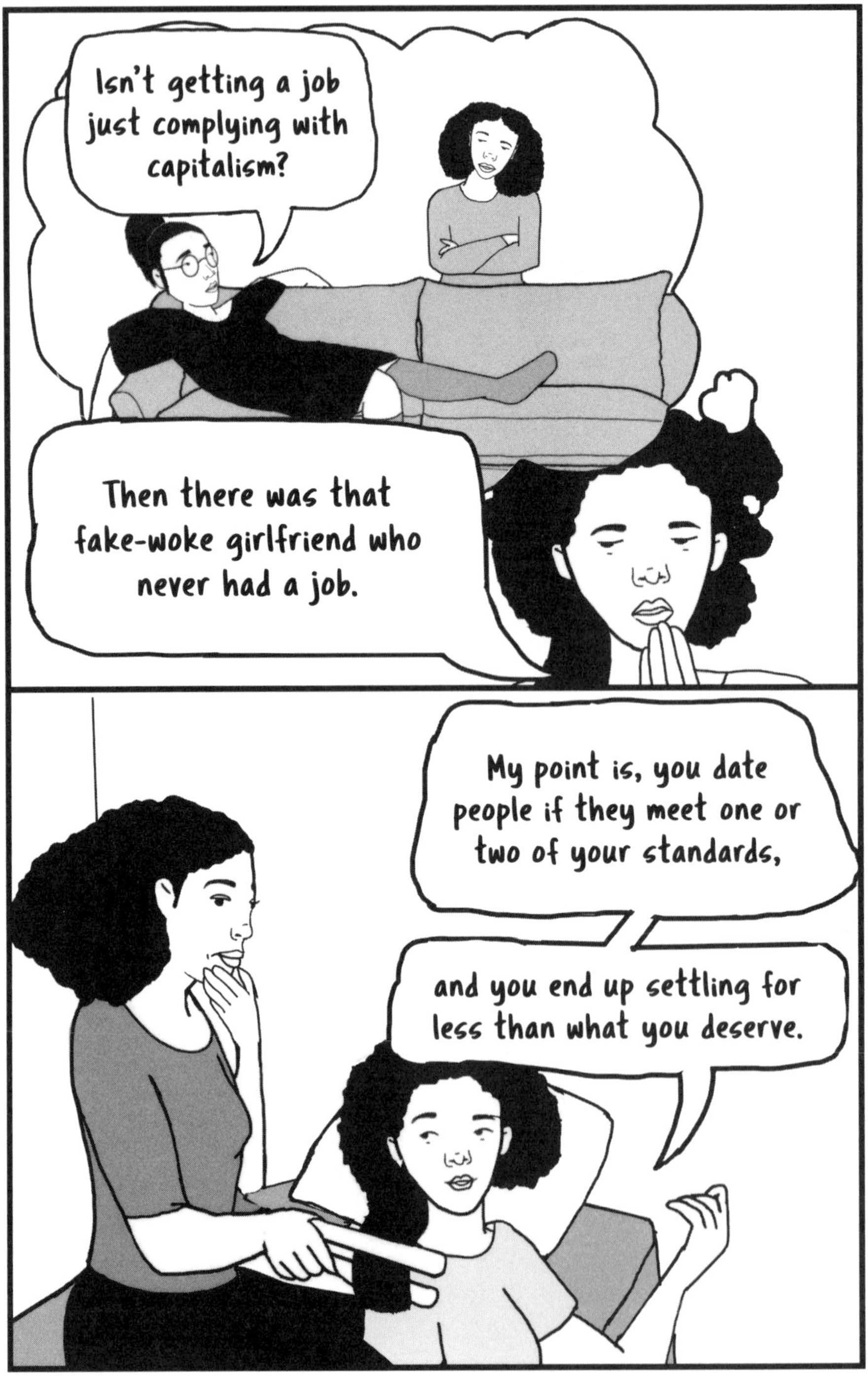
Isn't getting a job just complying with capitalism?
Then there was that fake-woke girlfriend who never had a job.
My point is, you date people if they meet one or two of your standards,
and you end up settling for less than what you deserve.

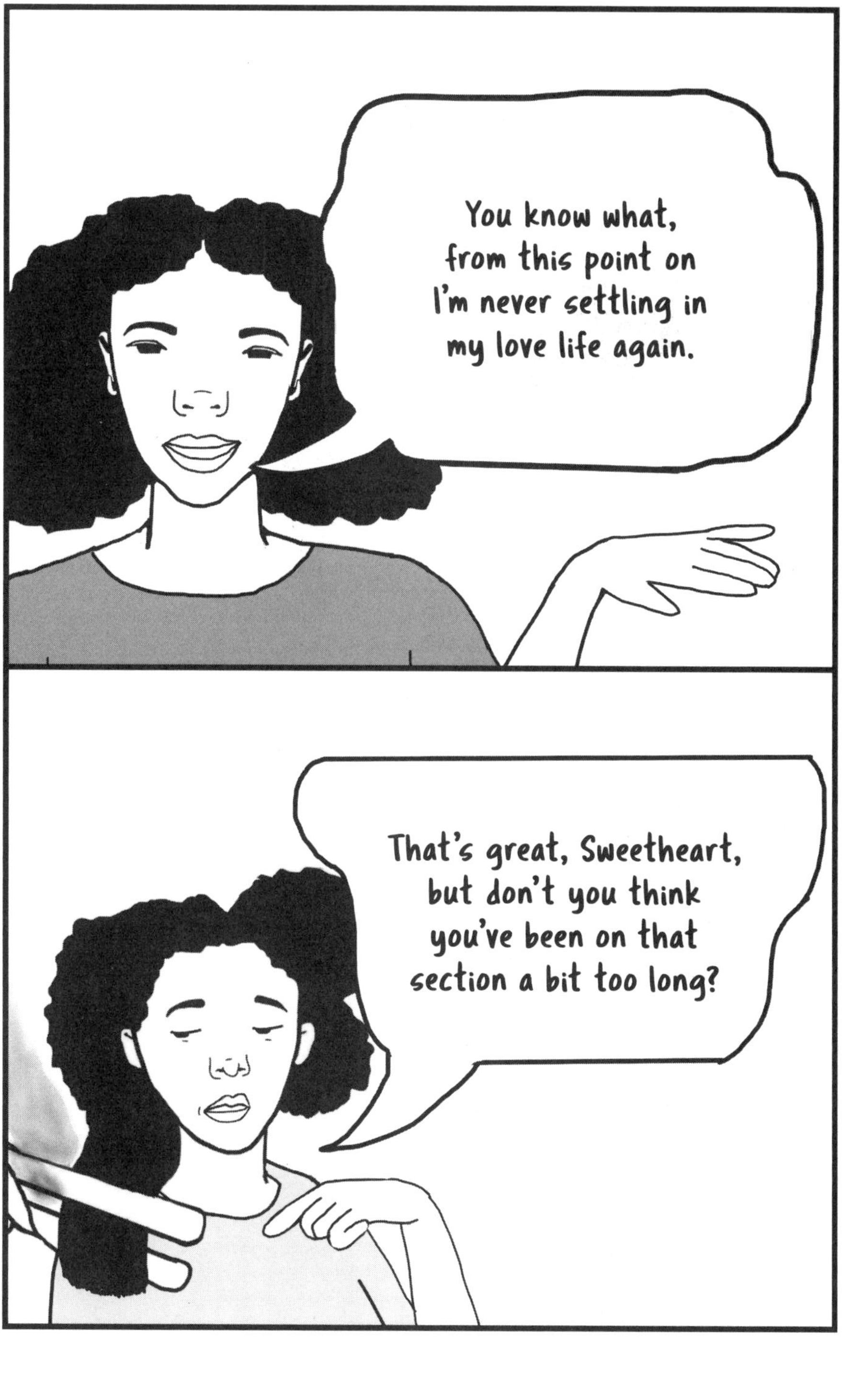
You know what, from this point on I'm never settling in my love life again.
That's great, Sweetheart, but don't you think you've been on that section a bit too long?

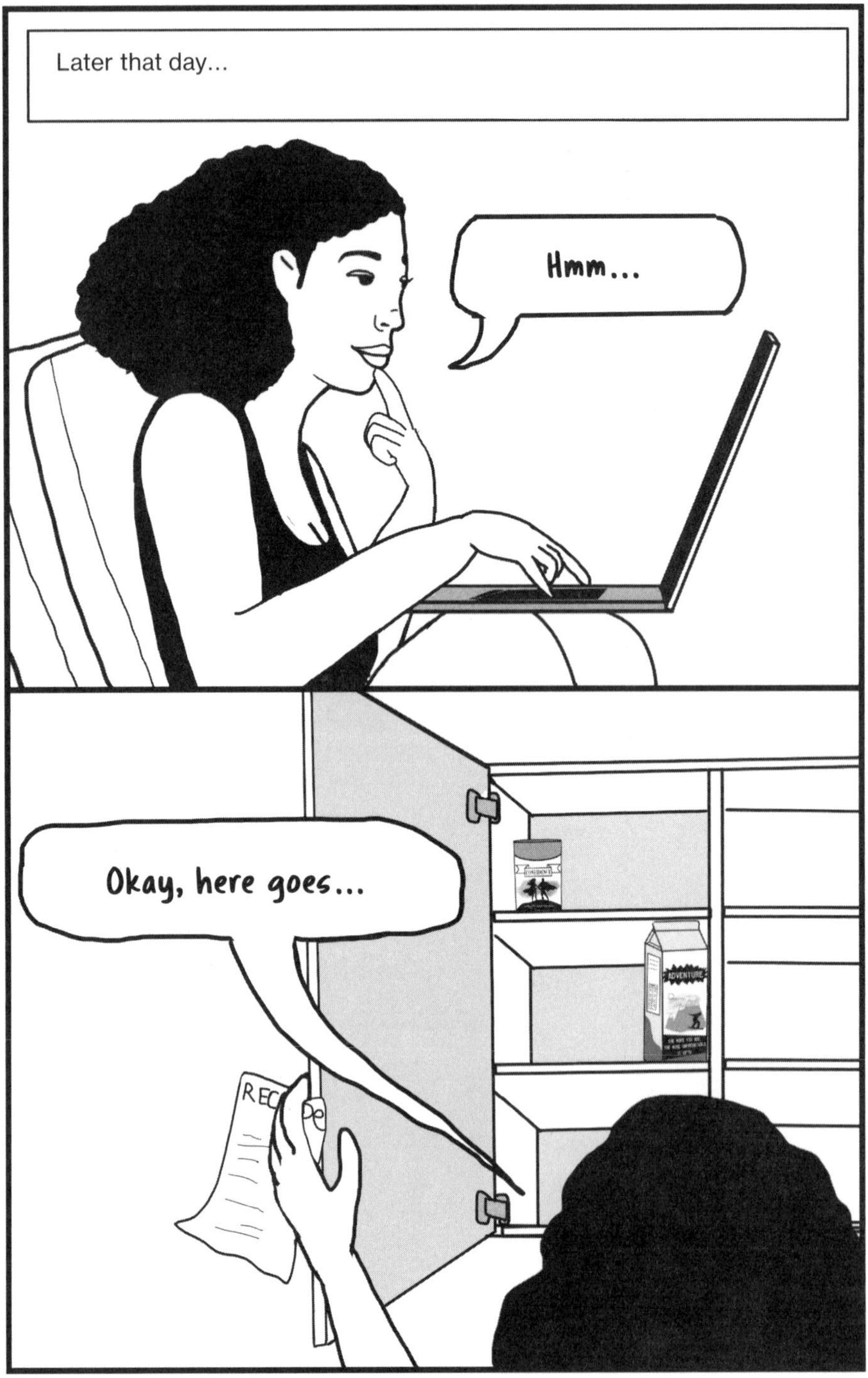
Later that day...
Hmm...
Okay, here goes...
ADVENTURE

A RECIPE FOR
THE PERFECT PARTNER:
A FOOLPROOF METHOD

Half a jar of empathy (Warning: Ensure it's from an authentic source.)

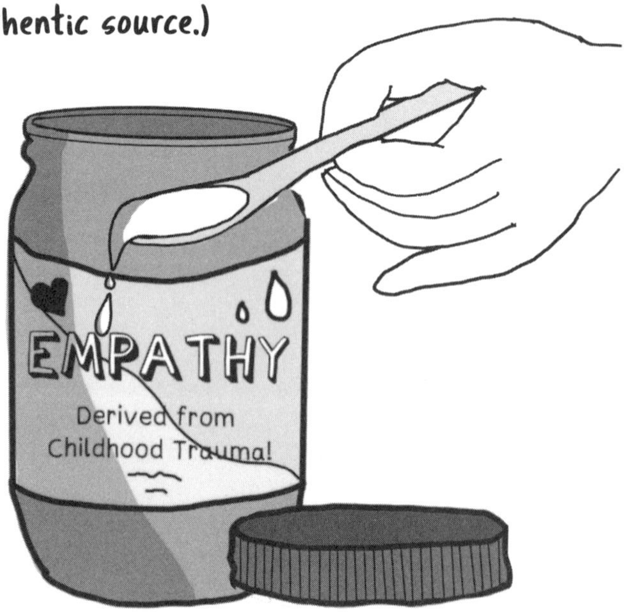
EMPATHY
Derived from Childhood Trauma!

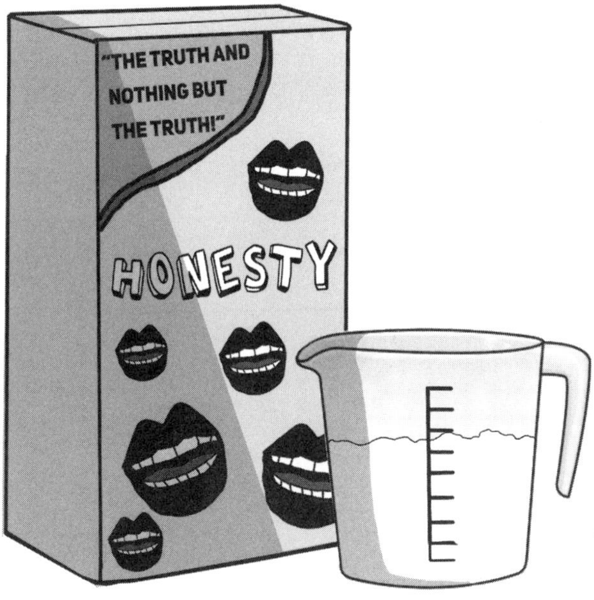
"THE TRUTH AND
NOTHING BUT
THE TRUTH!"
HONESTY

A healthy dose of honesty
(Add as much as you can handle.)

A few tablespoons of confidence

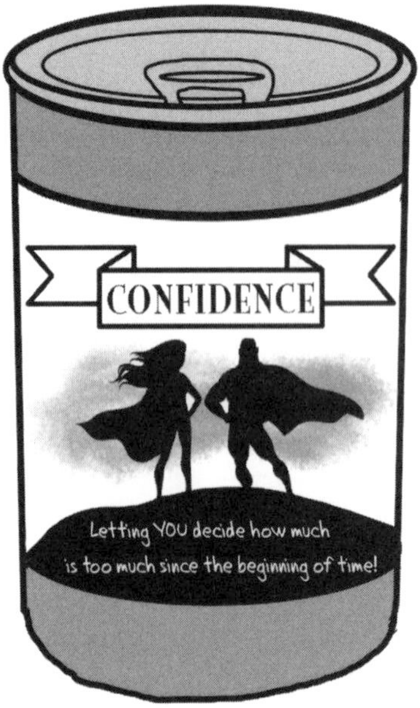
CONFIDENCE
Letting YOU decide how much
is too much since the beginning of time!

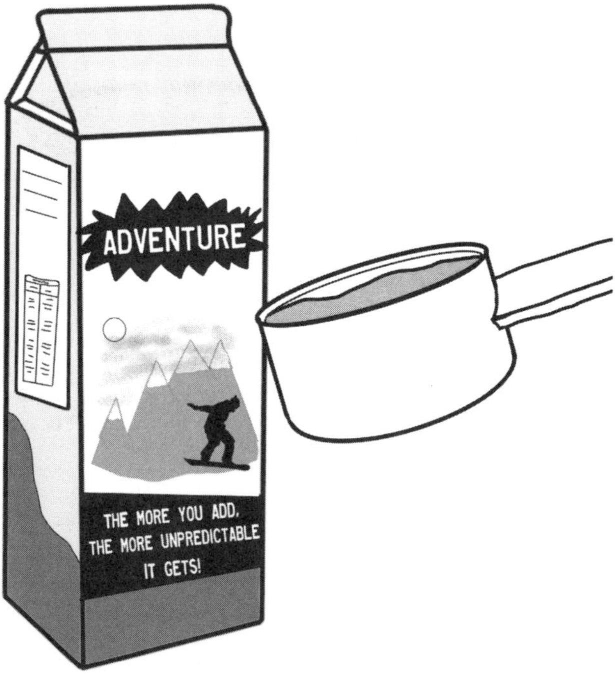
ADVENTURE
THE MORE YOU ADD,
THE MORE UNPREDICTABLE
IT GETS!

A cup of adventure

As many dollops of affection
as you can handle

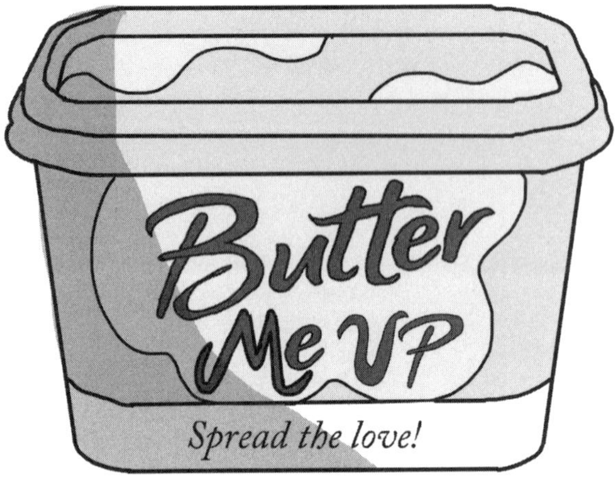
Butter Me Up
Spread the love!

AND...

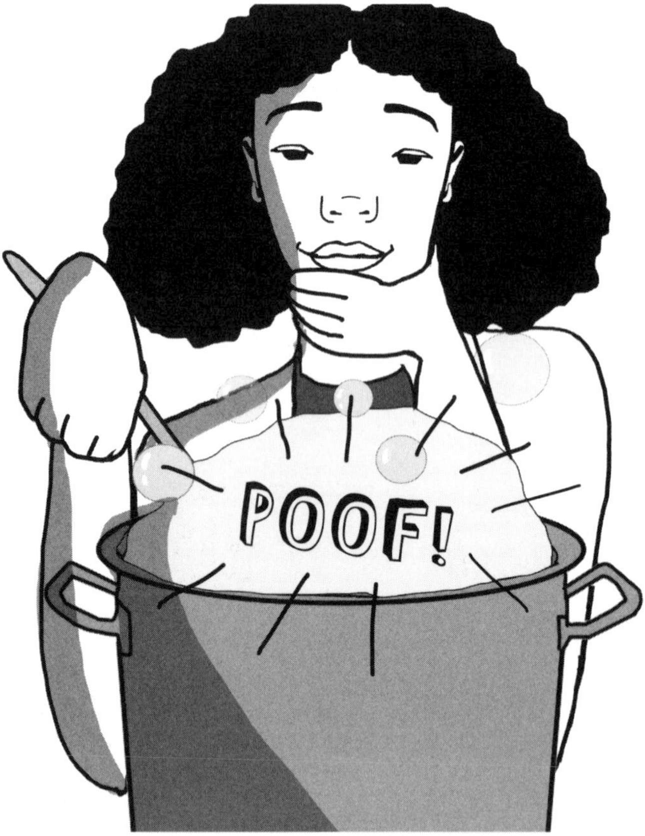
POOF!

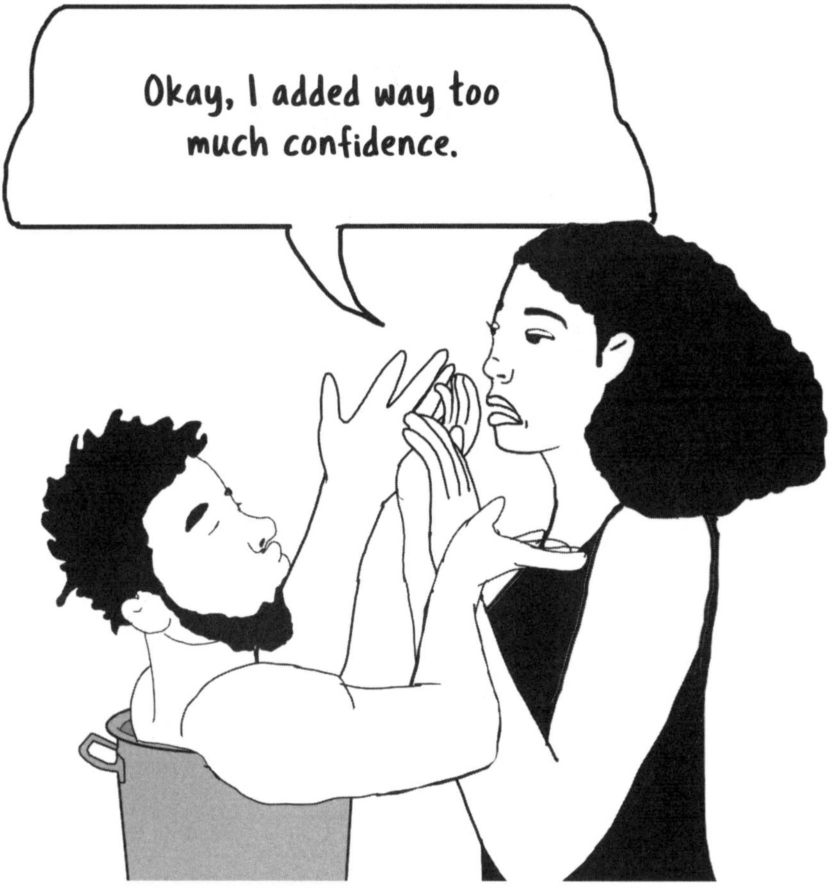
Okay, I added way too much confidence.

CHAPTER THREE

GOOD NEWS! THERE'S MORE THAN ONE

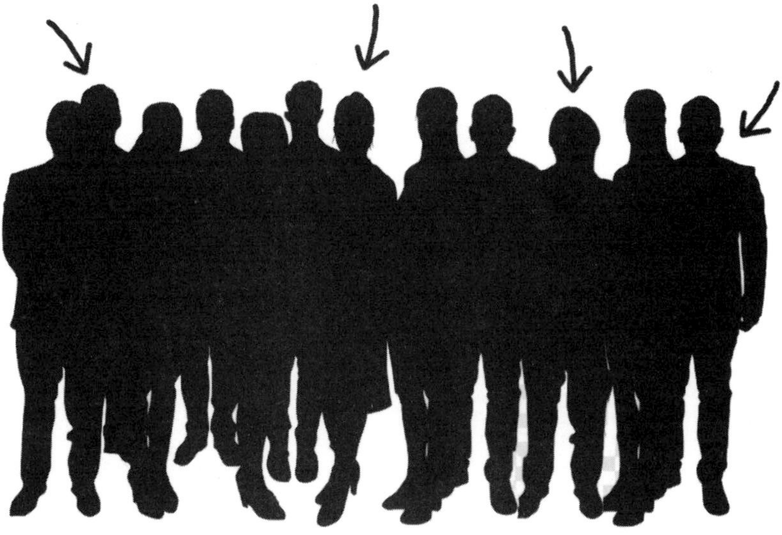

Good News! There's More Than One

We live on a planet consisting of almost eight billion people, yet we
are fixated on finding one specific person to be our so-called soul mate.
Many cultures have their own version of the soul mate: the one person
in the universe perfectly suited for them in every way imaginable. Aside
from adding a lot of pressure to dating, the concept of a soul mate also
significantly limits our choices—it's also arguably a relatively new social
concept. So what if instead we start with the assumption that multiple
people could be "the one"? It might change our approach to dating—
or even help us enjoy it!

In theory, the ideal partner, or   soul mate, is simply someone with whom
you share common interests, ideals, and values. In addition, the sex is great,
the conversations are vibrant, and the chemistry is intense. In short, this

person satisfies most of your desires in
a relationship. When we break it down
like this, finding "the one" is just about
partnering with a person you are highly
compatible with—not necessarily about
finding your one-and-only needle in the
haystack.

If your goal with dating is to enter into a serious monogamous relationship,
it's important to continually refer to your list of nonnegotiables, areas of
flexibility, and do-not-applies. You owe it to yourself not to settle for less
than what you deserve. However, it's important to note that the person
who meets your standards can come in many varieties. If you've previously
dated people with similar physical characteristics, how would it feel to
be more flexible about your preferences on appearance? While physical
appearance can spark the initial attraction to a person, the reality is that
how a person looks tells us very little about the qualities they bring to a
relationship or your compatibility with them. Think about dating people

of different races, heights, body types, or physical abilities. You will widen your dating pool and better your chances of finding what you're looking for. With a more open mind, you might find that you'll meet many more people with whom you're highly compatible.

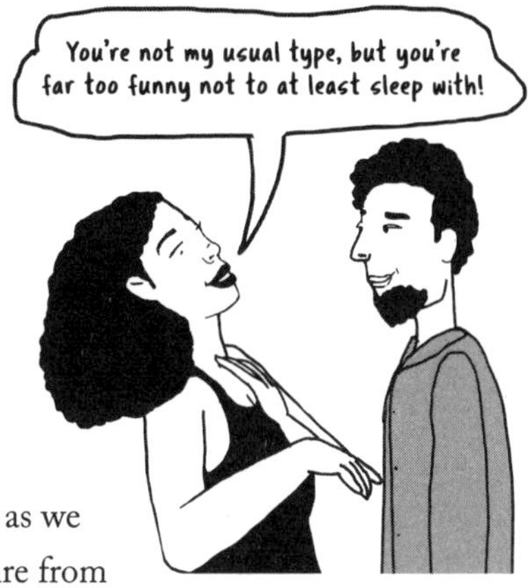
You're not my usual type, but you're far too funny not to at least sleep with!

The most compelling argument against the notion that there is a single person out there for you—your one-and-only soul mate—is that as we grow and evolve, what we need, expect, and desire from a partner changes and grows too. Someone compatible with you now may be so only for a certain period in your life. Why do you think so many breakups, divorces, and relationship problems happen? People can change, and couples may be unable to adapt to each other for various reasons. When this happens, it's time to move on and update your list of wants. What you want in your twenties could be completely different from what you want in your thirties. And the people you dated ten years ago might be completely different from the people you date now. Someone may have met your standards a year ago, but now you realize those standards no longer apply. Things change, and so do you.

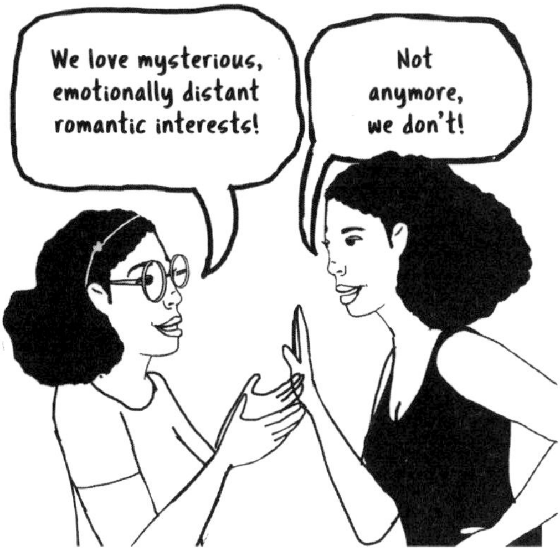
We love mysterious, emotionally distant romantic interests!
Not anymore, we don't!

The key here is to focus less on finding the idealized "one" and instead be open to meeting someone with whom you're compatible now and who treats you the way you deserve to be treated. As you date, have fun getting to know each individual for who they are, while also asking yourself if the two of you are both compatible and adaptable. If you find someone you are attracted to, with whom you share important core values, and who chooses to love, respect, value, and support you, then it sounds like you've found someone, perhaps one of many people, with whom you're compatible. This is the beginning of a healthy relationship.

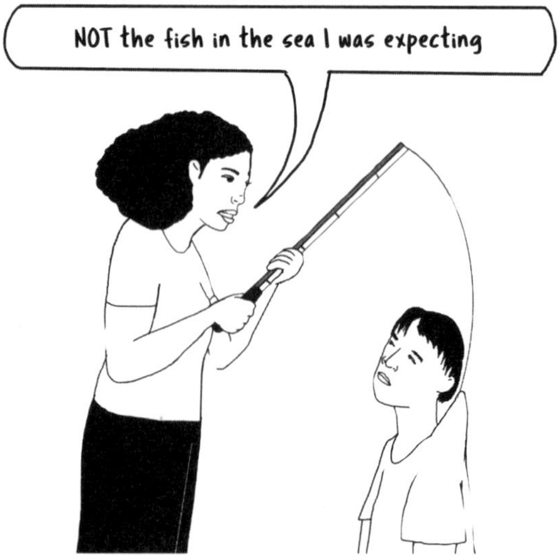
NOT the fish in the sea I was expecting

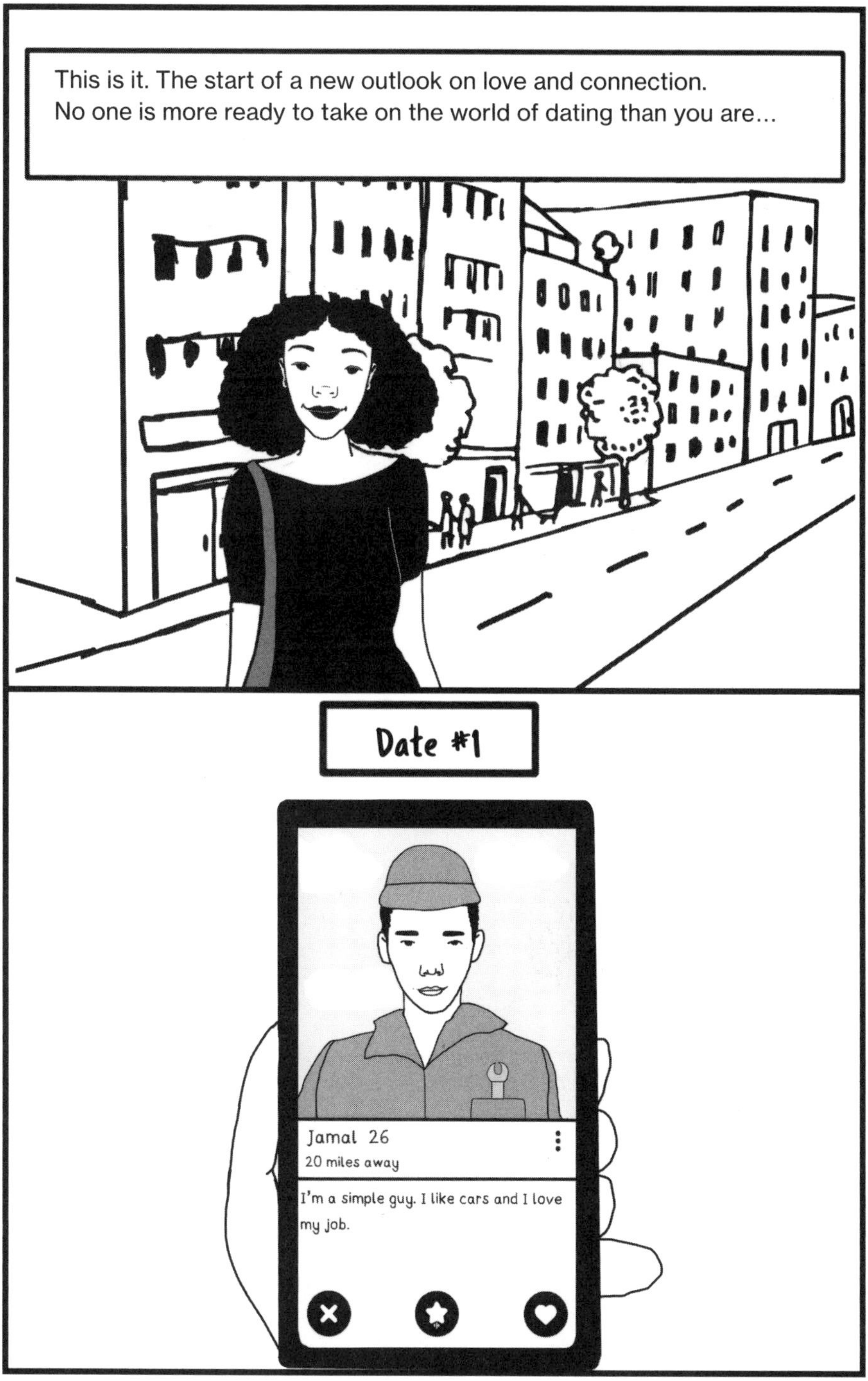
This is it. The start of a new outlook on love and connection.
No one is more ready to take on the world of dating than you are...
Date #1
Jamal 26
20 miles away
I'm a simple guy. I like cars and I love my job.

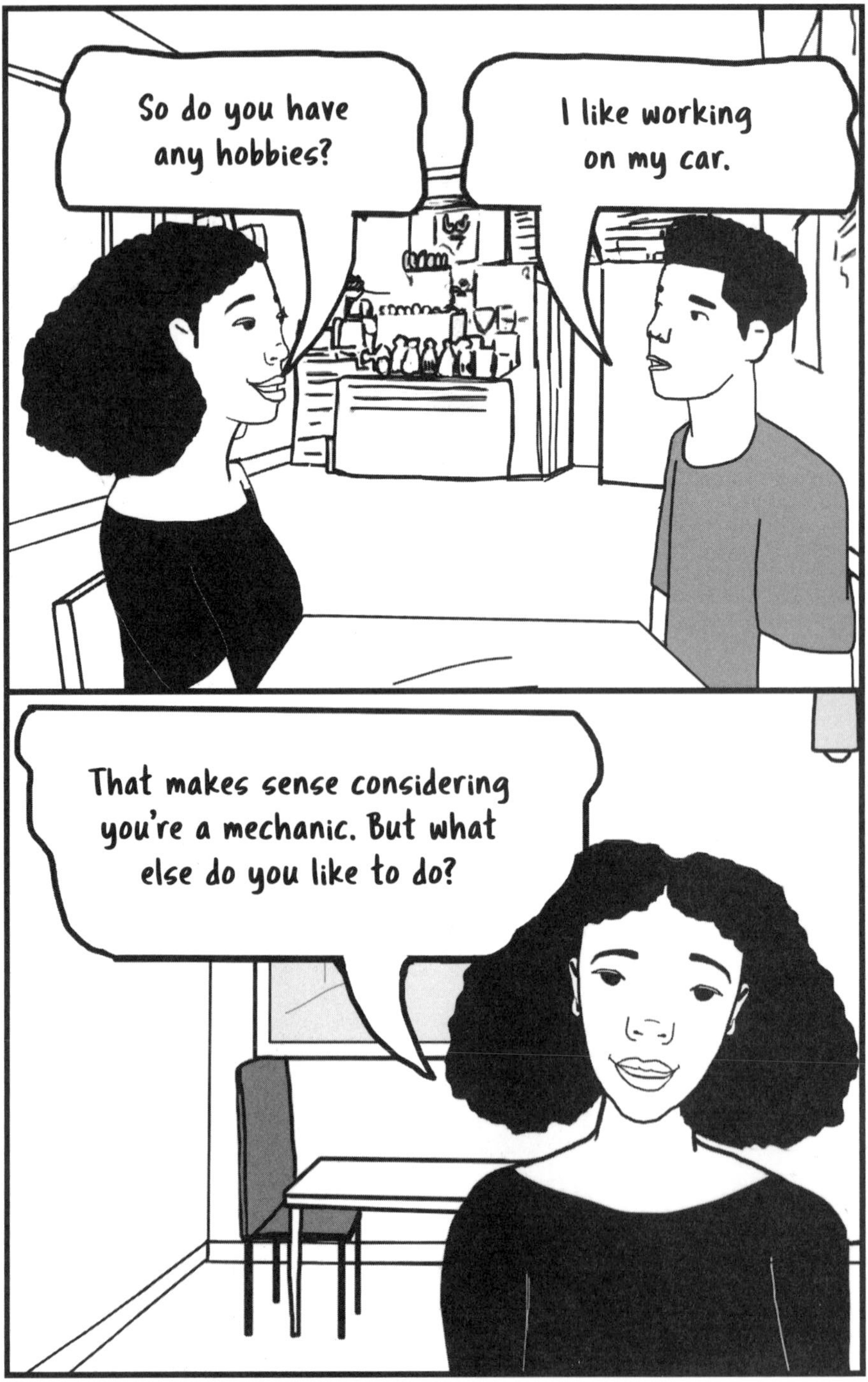
So do you have any hobbies?
I like working on my car.
That makes sense considering you're a mechanic. But what else do you like to do?

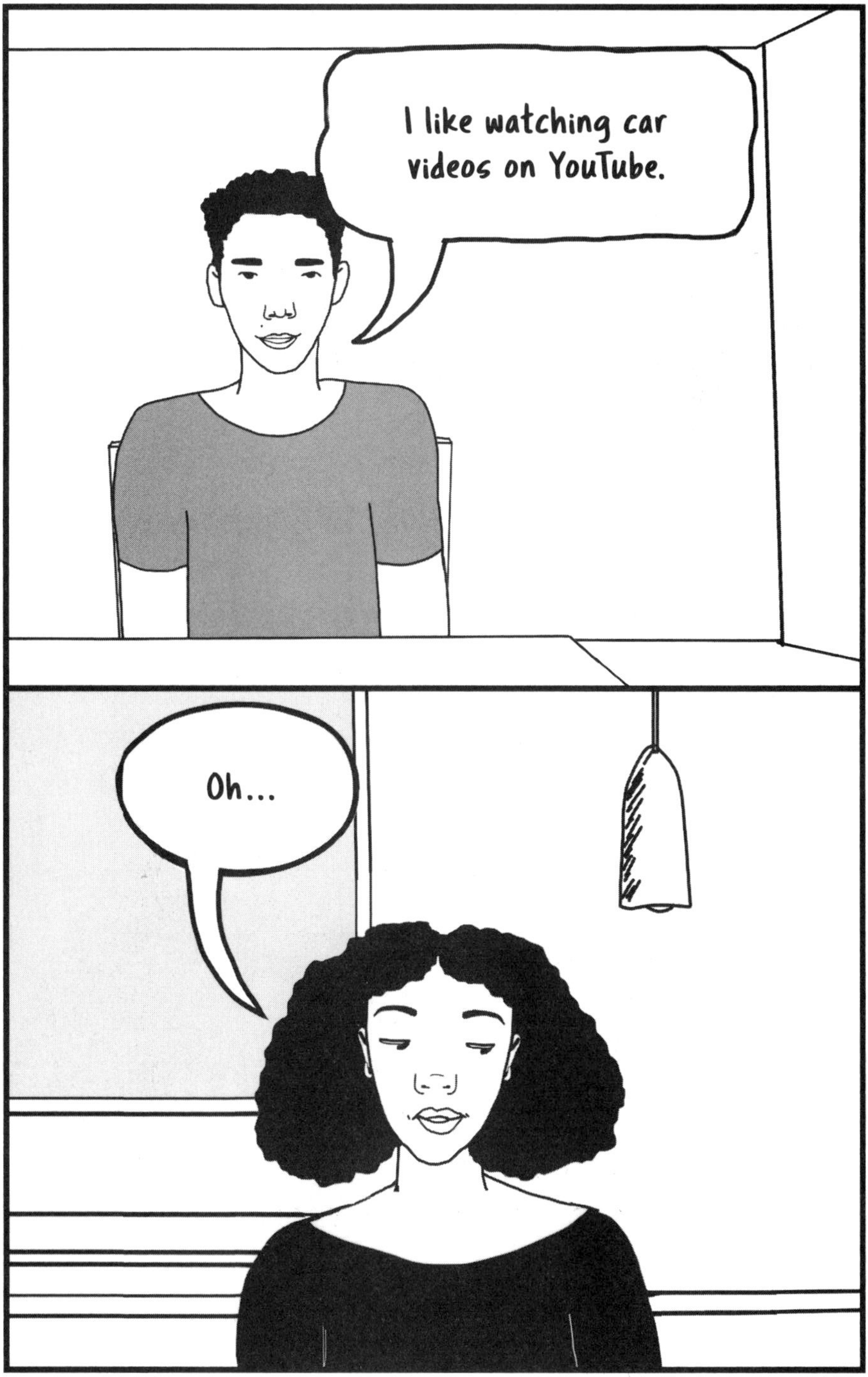
I like watching car videos on YouTube.
Oh...

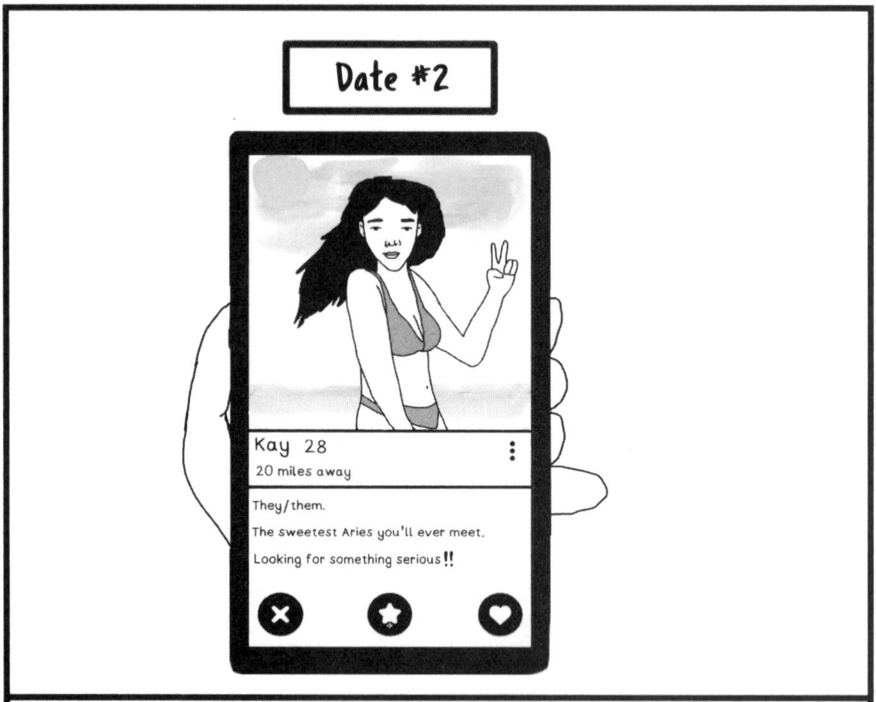
Date #2
Kay 28
20 miles away
They/them.
The sweetest Aries you'll ever meet.
Looking for something serious!!

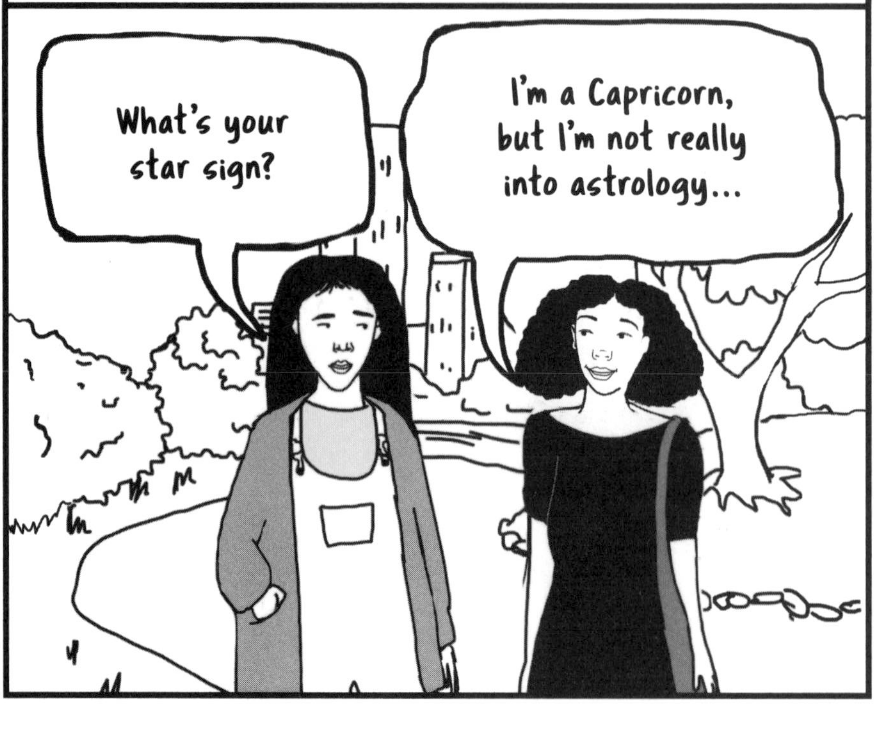
What's your star sign?
I'm a Capricorn, but I'm not really into astrology...

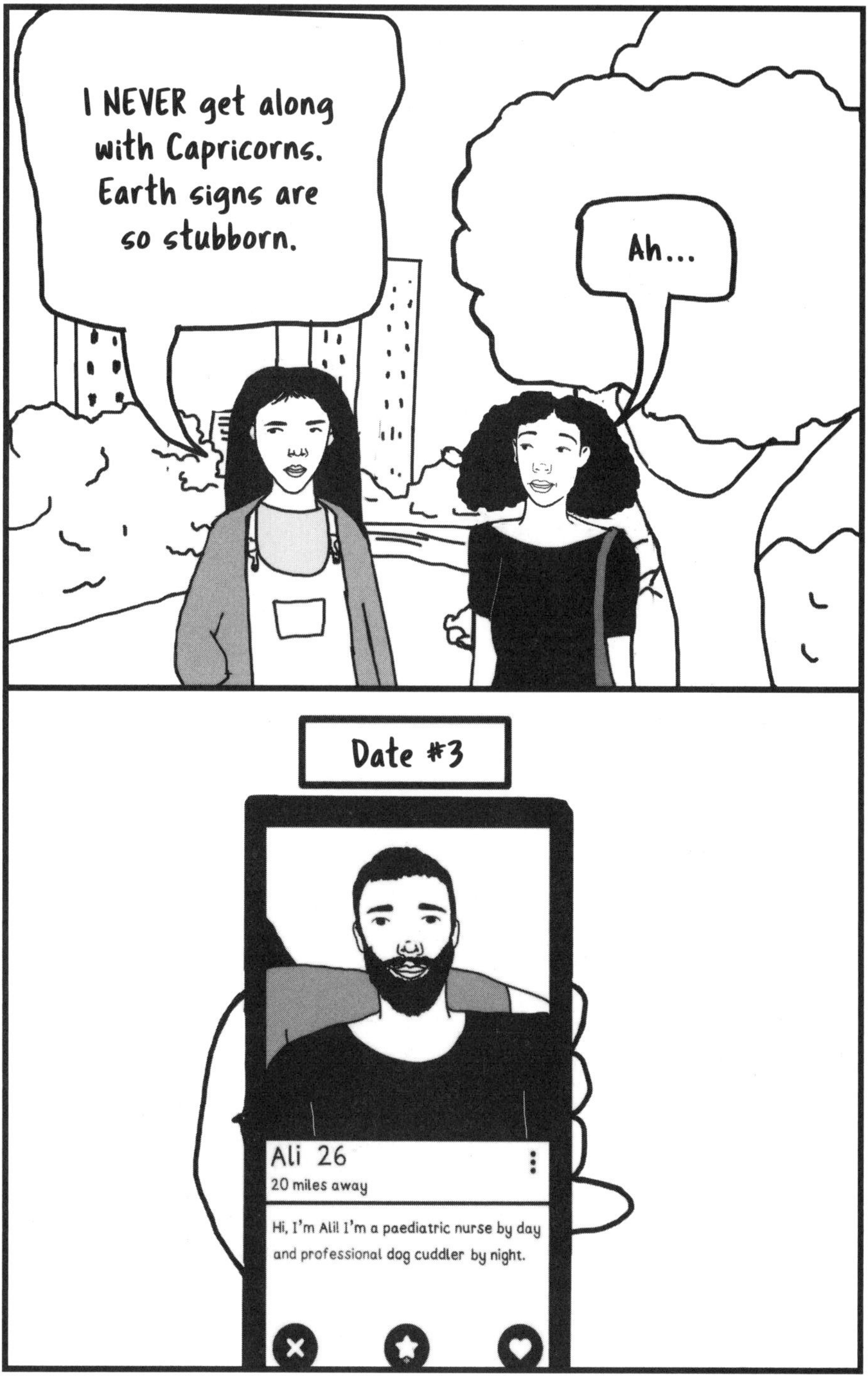
I NEVER get along with Capricorns. Earth signs are so stubborn.
Ah...
Date #3
Ali 26
20 miles away
Hi, I'm Ali! I'm a paediatric nurse by day and professional dog cuddler by night.

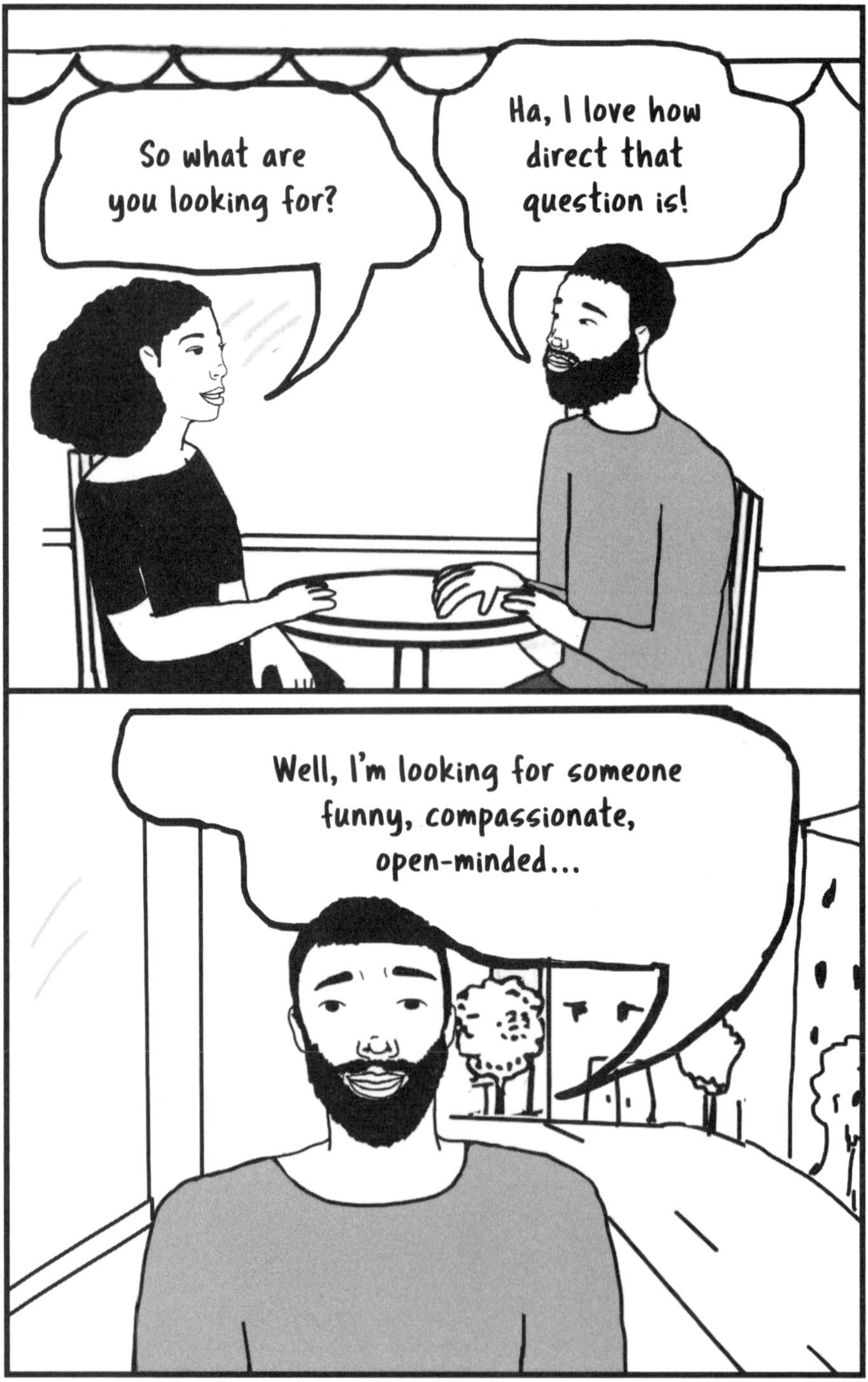
So what are you looking for?
Ha, I love how direct that question is!
Well, I'm looking for someone funny, compassionate, open-minded...

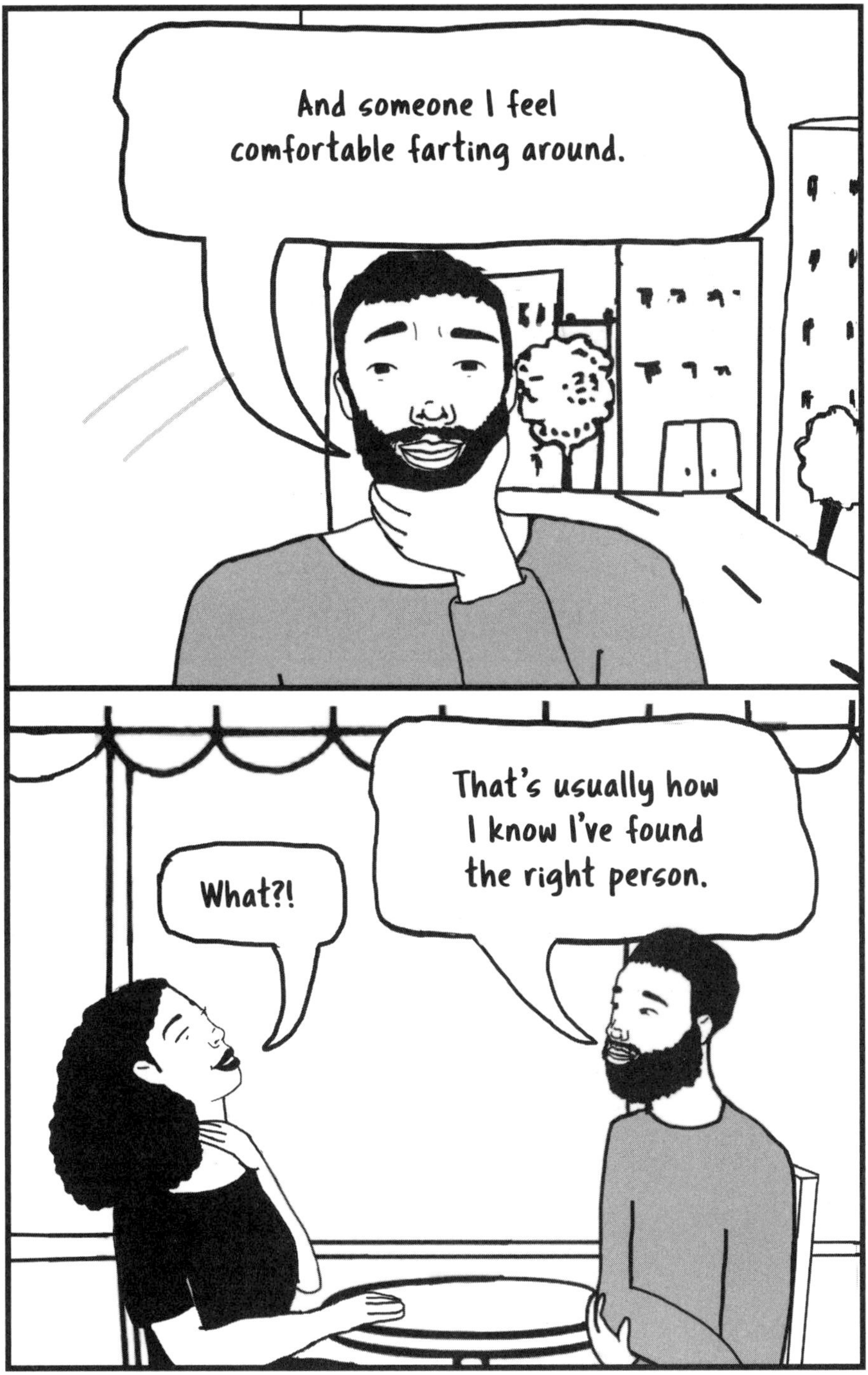
And someone I feel comfortable farting around.
What?!
That's usually how I know I've found the right person.

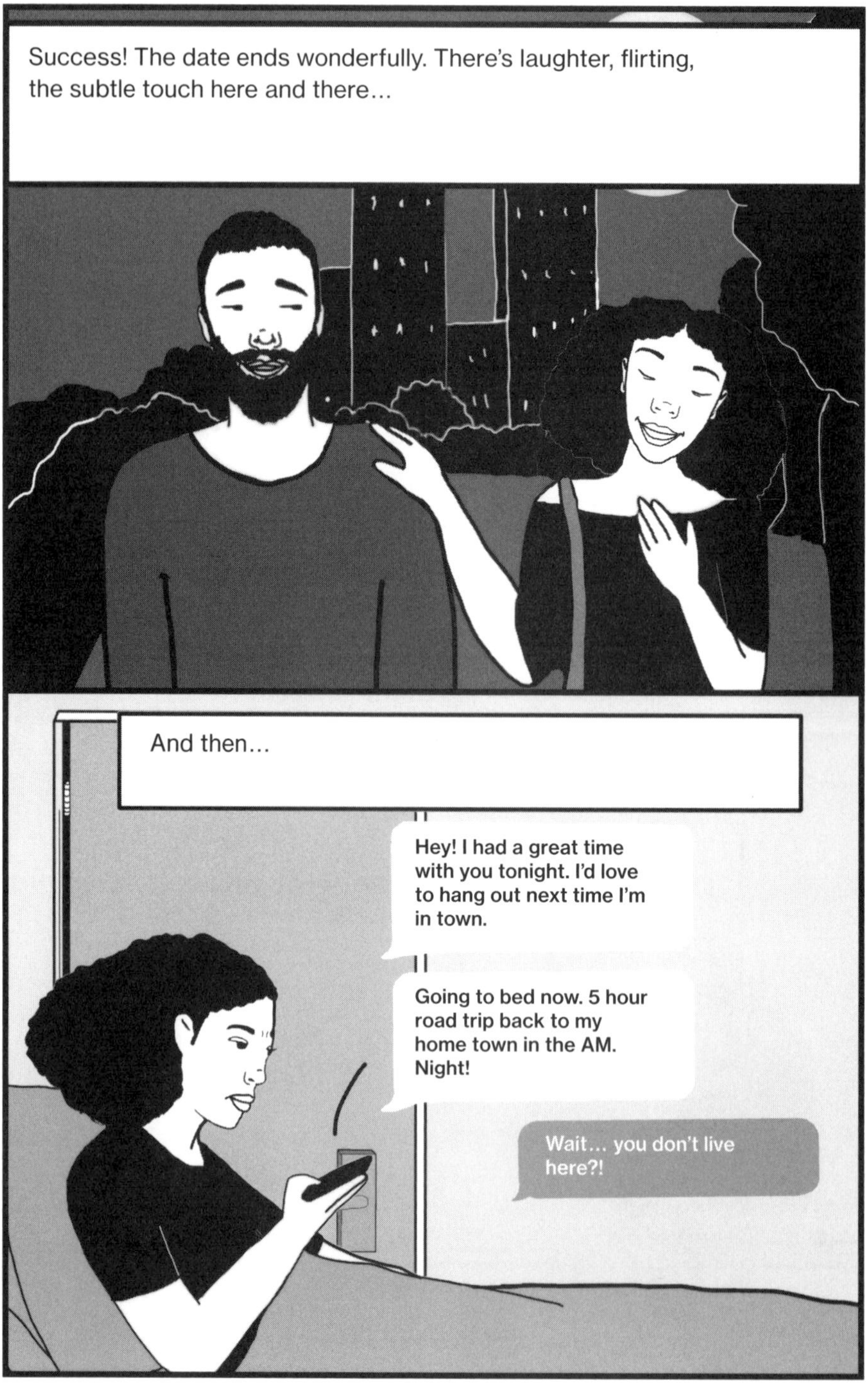
Success! The date ends wonderfully. There's laughter, flirting, the subtle touch here and there...
And then...
Hey! I had a great time with you tonight. I'd love to hang out next time I'm in town.
Going to bed now. 5 hour road trip back to my home town in the AM. Night!
Wait... you don't live here?!

THE OTHER
FIVE LOVE LANGUAGES

1. Physical Distance

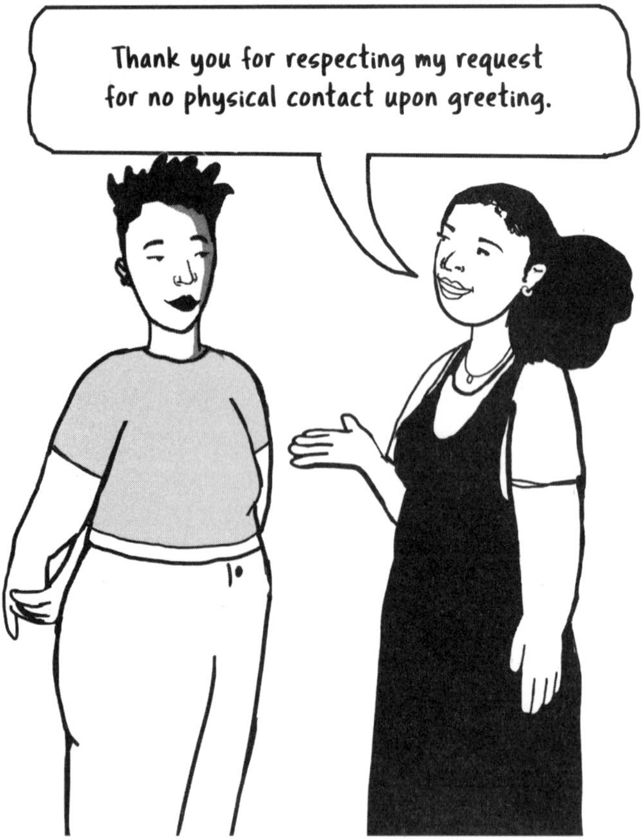
Thank you for respecting my request for no physical contact upon greeting.

2. Quality Silent Time

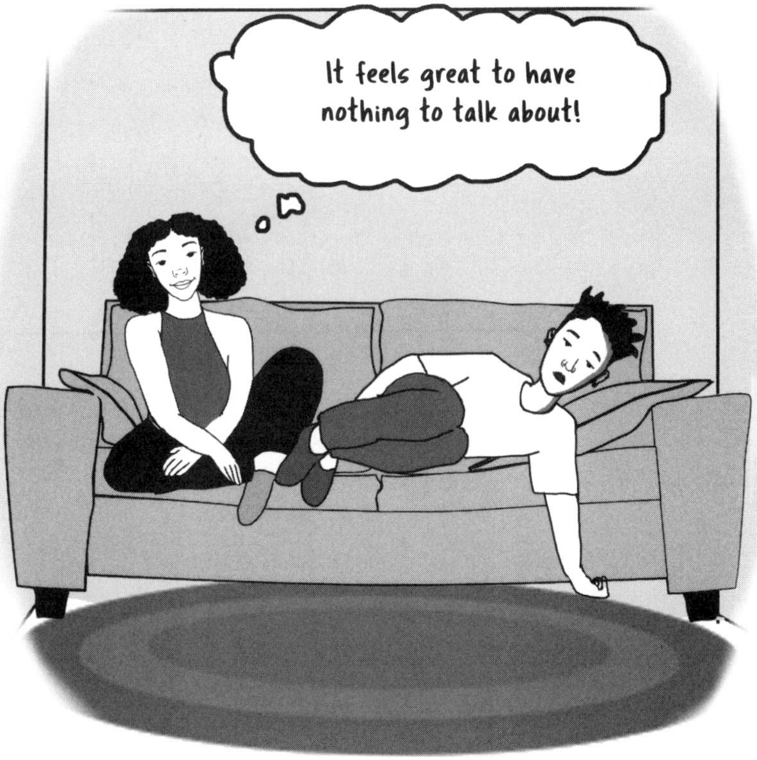
It feels great to have nothing to talk about!

3. Words of Education

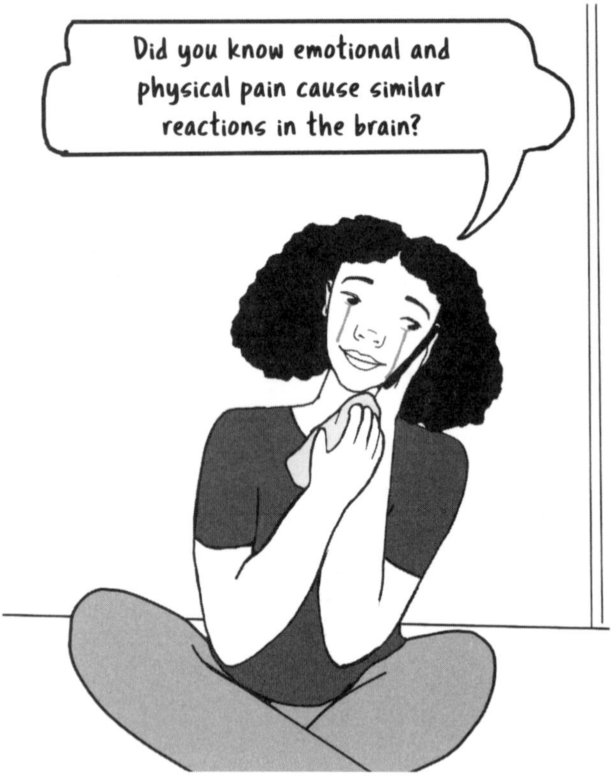
Did you know emotional and physical pain cause similar reactions in the brain?

4. Acts That Serve Us

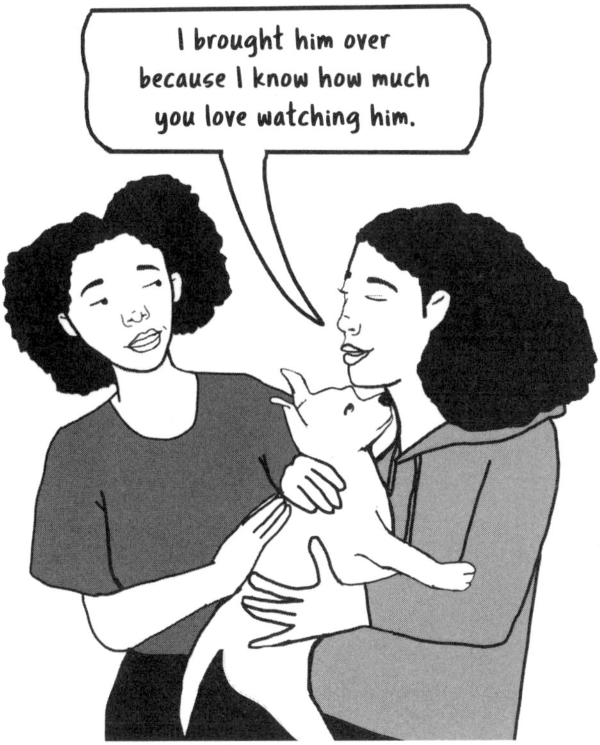
I brought him over because I know how much you love watching him.

5. Edible Gifts

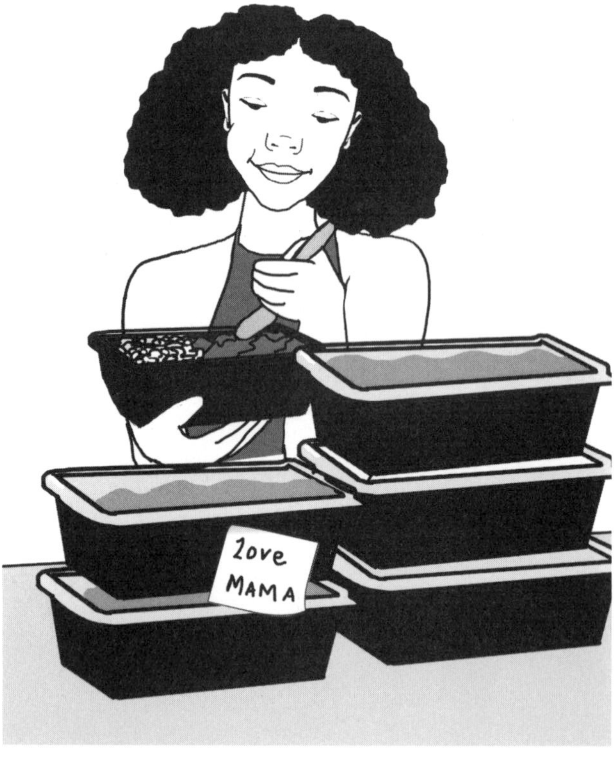

love
MAMA

—

Are they
mysterious
or just
really bad at
communication?

—

CHAPTER FOUR

WHY YOU NEED TO DATE YOURSELF

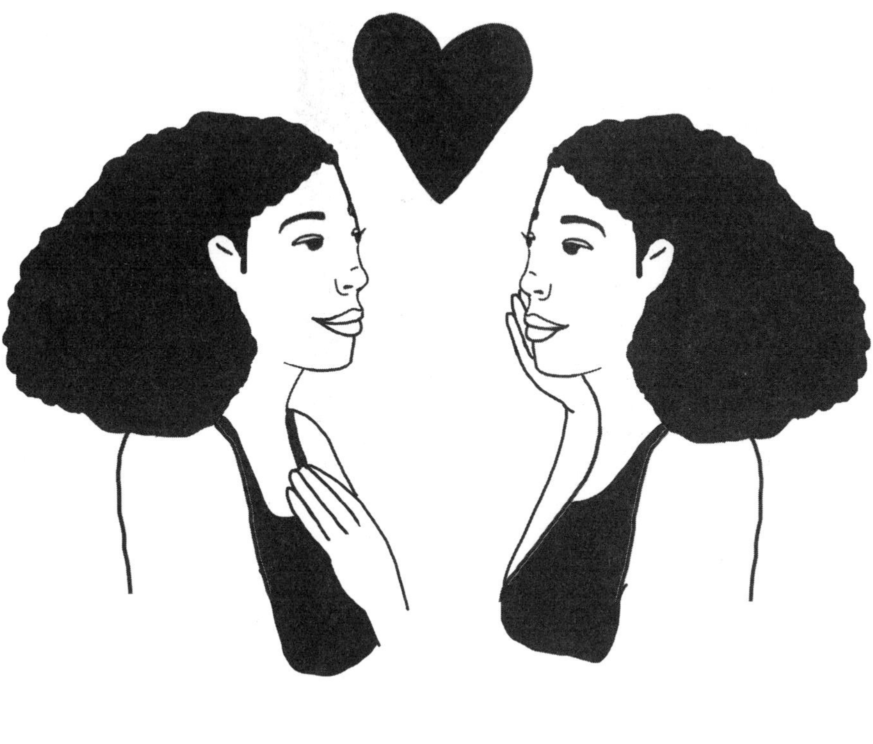

Why You Need to Date Yourself

Self-
actualization
Self-esteem
Love & belonging
Safety
Physiological needs

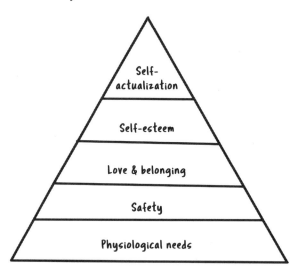

If you've never heard the expression "date yourself," then are you even a frustrated young adult who has consumed a lifetime's worth of love and relationship advice? The concept of dating yourself suggests we've reached a point culturally where the struggle to meet someone is so significant that we must turn to ourselves for true love. But what's the harm in developing a relationship with yourself that reflects how you intend to be treated in a relationship? Doing so can be a great way to a) figure out what you want in a partner and b) help manage feelings of loneliness and desperation.

There are many theories for why humans seek companionship. The need for love is the third level of Maslow's hierarchy of needs—humans literally need it to survive. We need all kinds of love in many different forms and not just from our romantic partners—we need to have intimacy, trust, and affection from our friends, family, and pets, too. However, sometimes the love we forget we need is love from ourselves. Loving ourselves makes it easier to recognize and process the love we receive from others.

So what does dating yourself even look like? It starts with getting to know yourself on a deeper level to develop a greater sense of self-love.

Loving yourself includes the everyday choices that make you feel happy and taken care of. It could be spending time at home on a Saturday night, enjoying a long, warm bath instead of lying down on your bed, scrolling through social media or dating apps. You could add some essential oils or a bath bomb, play your favorite music, and light a few candles for a more sensual experience. Afterward, moisturize your whole body with your best lotion. This is a great way to feel intimate and well taken care of, a feeling everyone deserves to experience on a regular basis. There's no need to wait until you're in a relationship.

Self-love doesn't stop at warm baths and body lotion. It's also doing the tough things, like swapping junk food for a nutritious meal, exercising regularly, or processing difficult thoughts and emotions through therapy or journaling. This is the side of self-love that's often less spoken about, and that may be because it's far less glamorous. Part of self-love is breaking old, harmful patterns so that we can give ourselves what we truly need to thrive.

Embarking on a meaningful relationship with yourself could also involve taking yourself on a "first date." That's right, just like a real date, where you get all dressed up and go to a nice venue and really get to *know* someone— except that someone is yourself. It might sound sad and lonely, but trust me—it's one of the best habits you can start for yourself. Learning to spend quality time with yourself is a great way to embrace solitude, gain a healthy sense of independence, and set the bar for what you expect to experience on a date with a potential partner.

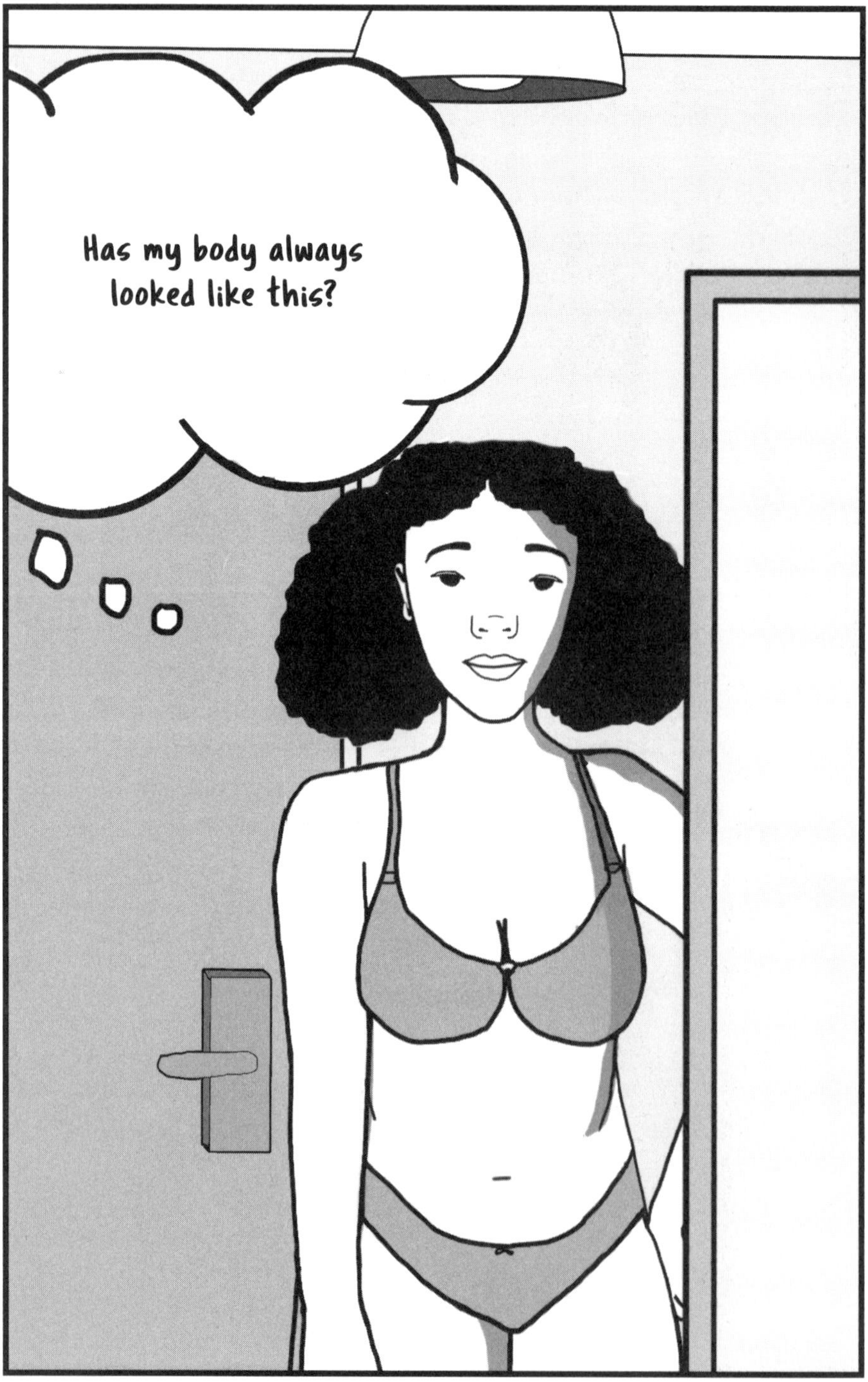
Has my body always looked like this?

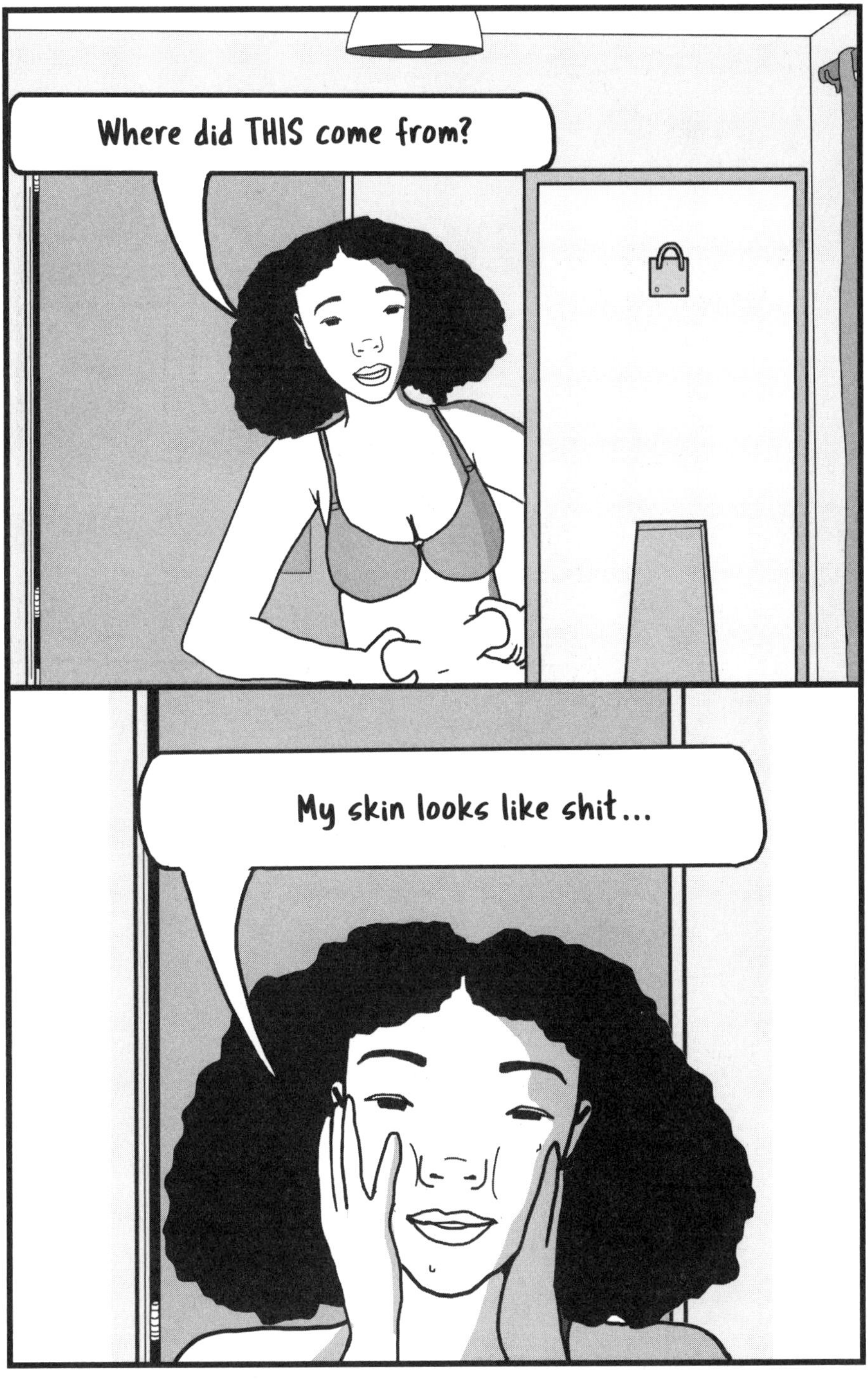
Where did THIS come from?
My skin looks like shit...

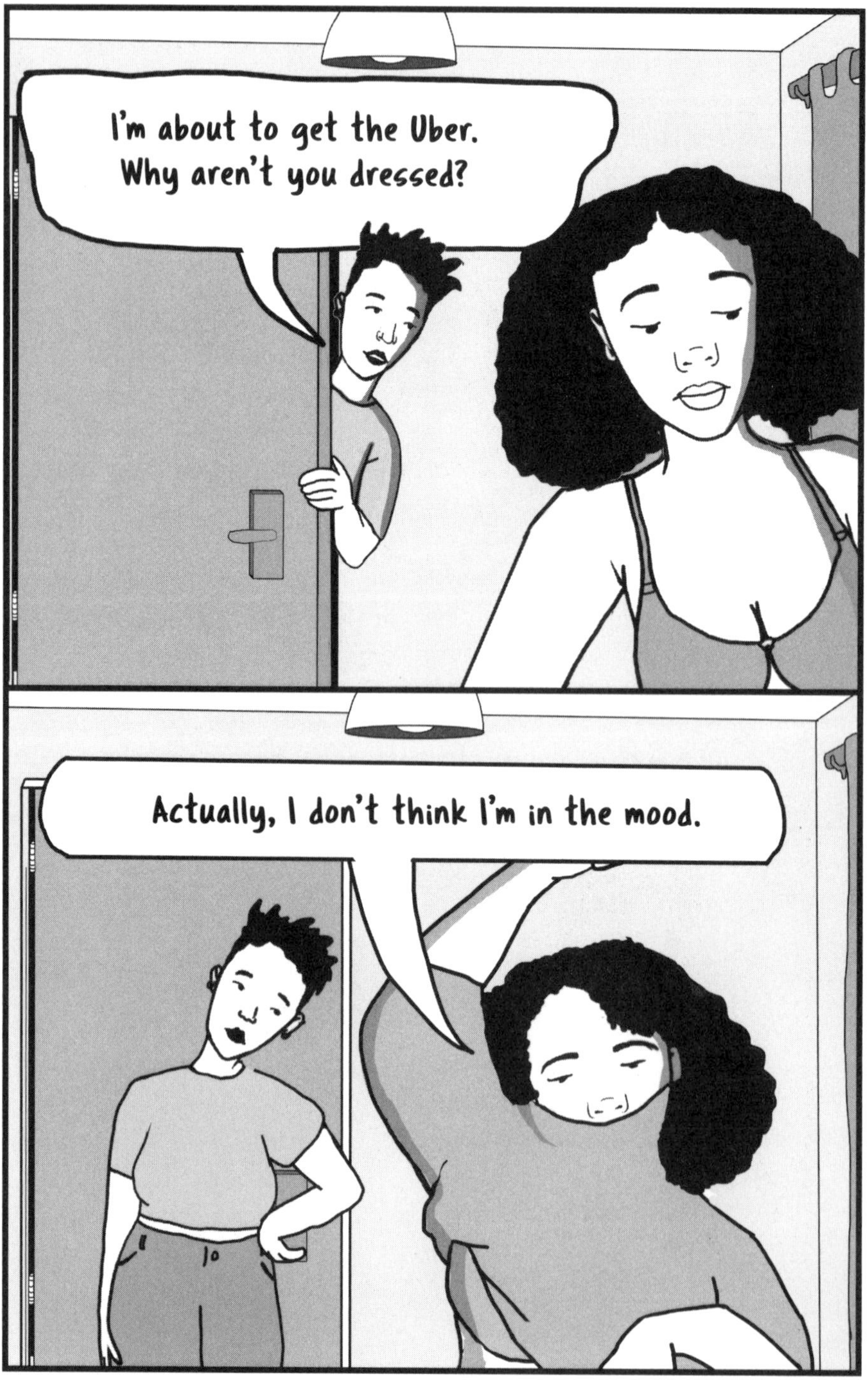
I'm about to get the Uber. Why aren't you dressed?
Actually, I don't think I'm in the mood.

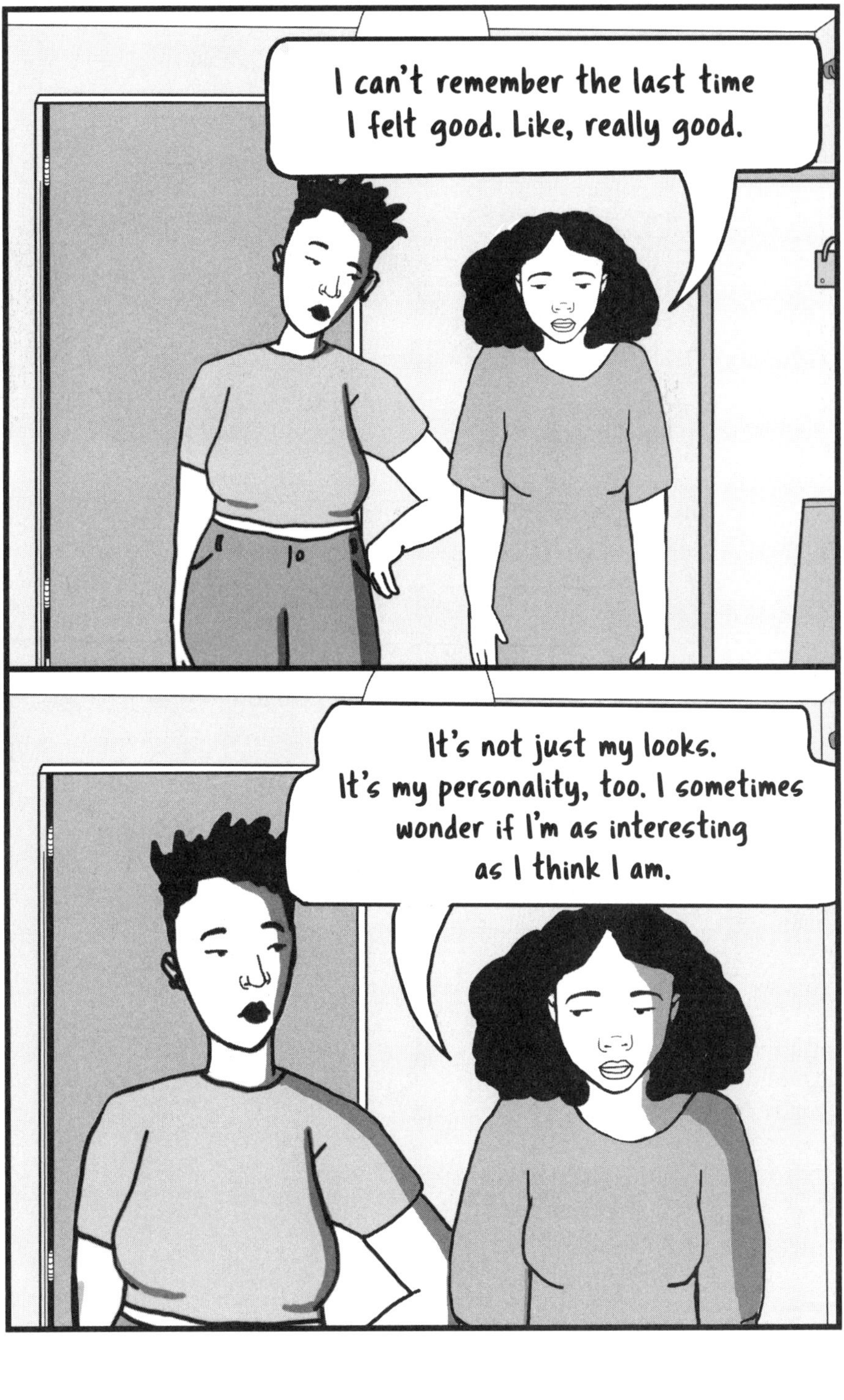
I can't remember the last time I felt good. Like, really good.
It's not just my looks. It's my personality, too. I sometimes wonder if I'm as interesting as I think I am.

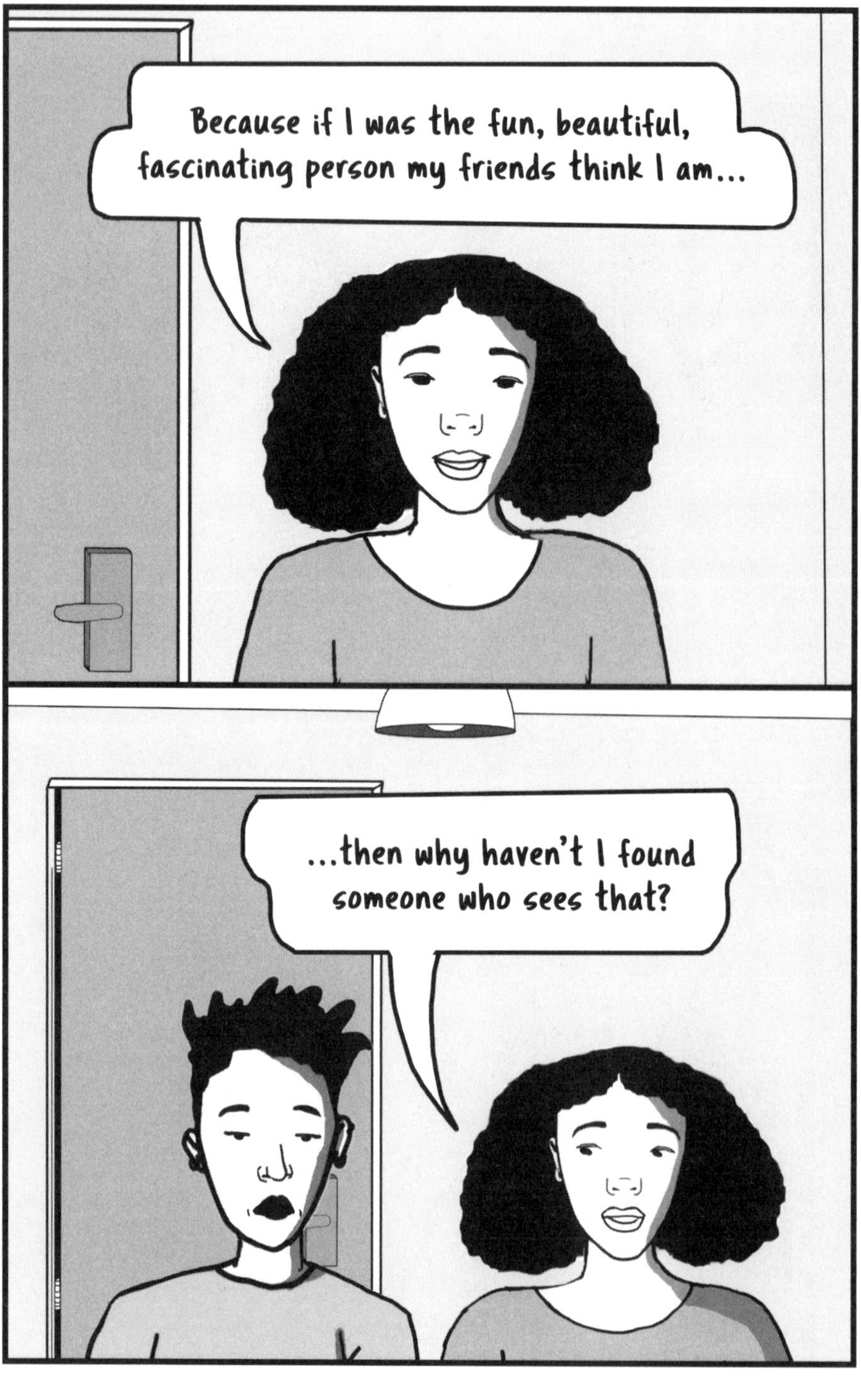
Because if I was the fun, beautiful, fascinating person my friends think I am...
...then why haven't I found someone who sees that?

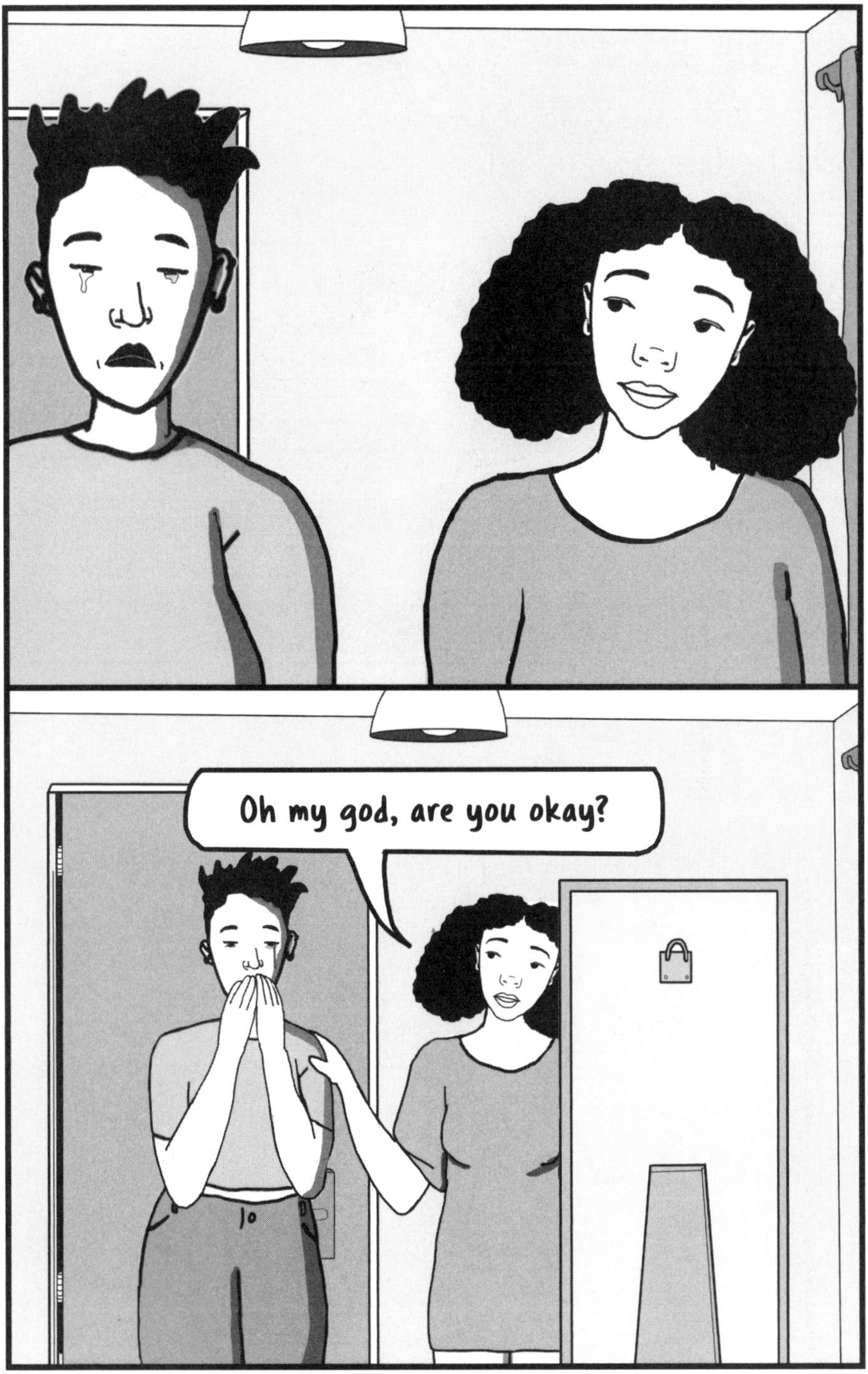
Oh my god, are you okay?

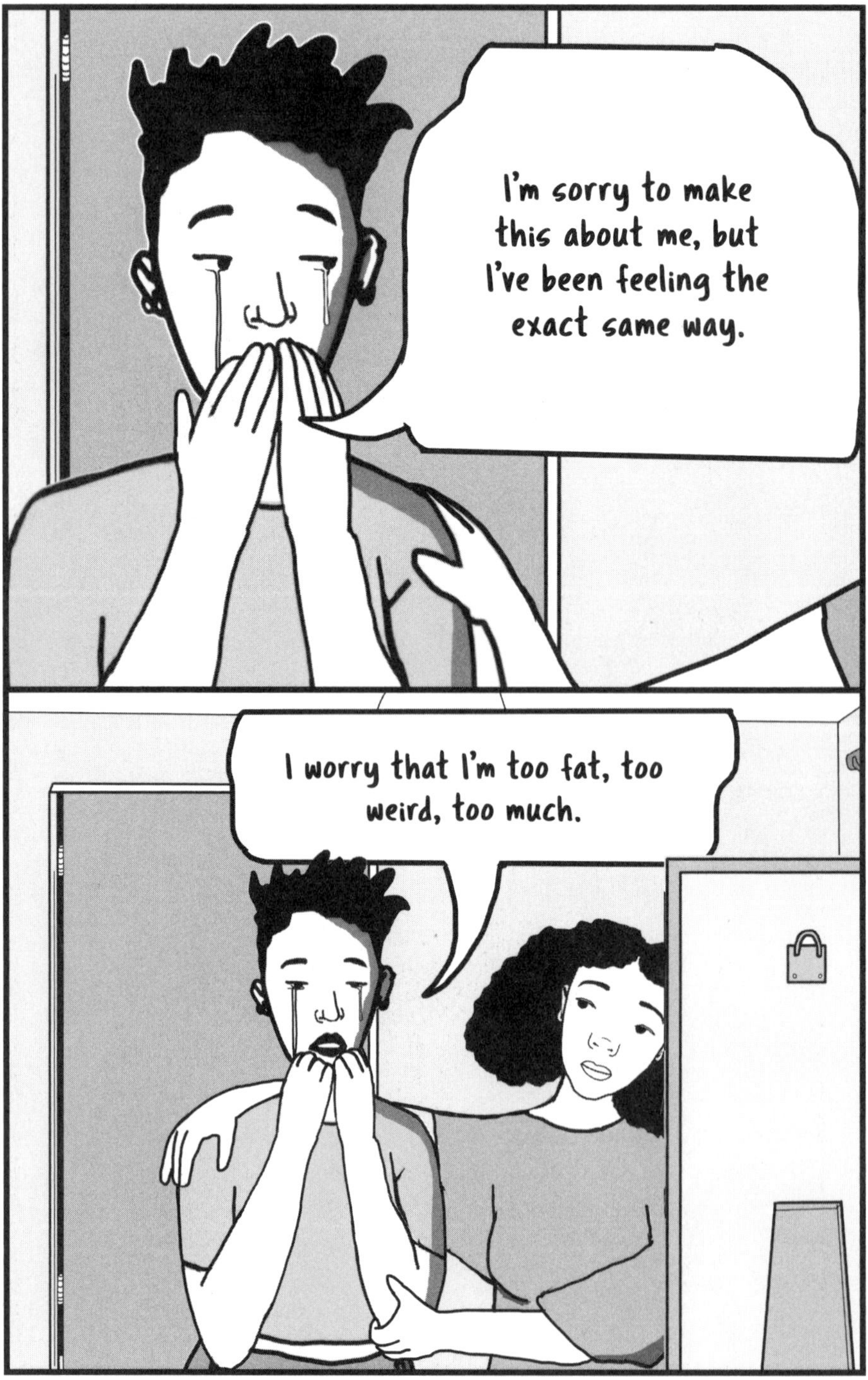
I'm sorry to make this about me, but I've been feeling the exact same way.
I worry that I'm too fat, too weird, too much.

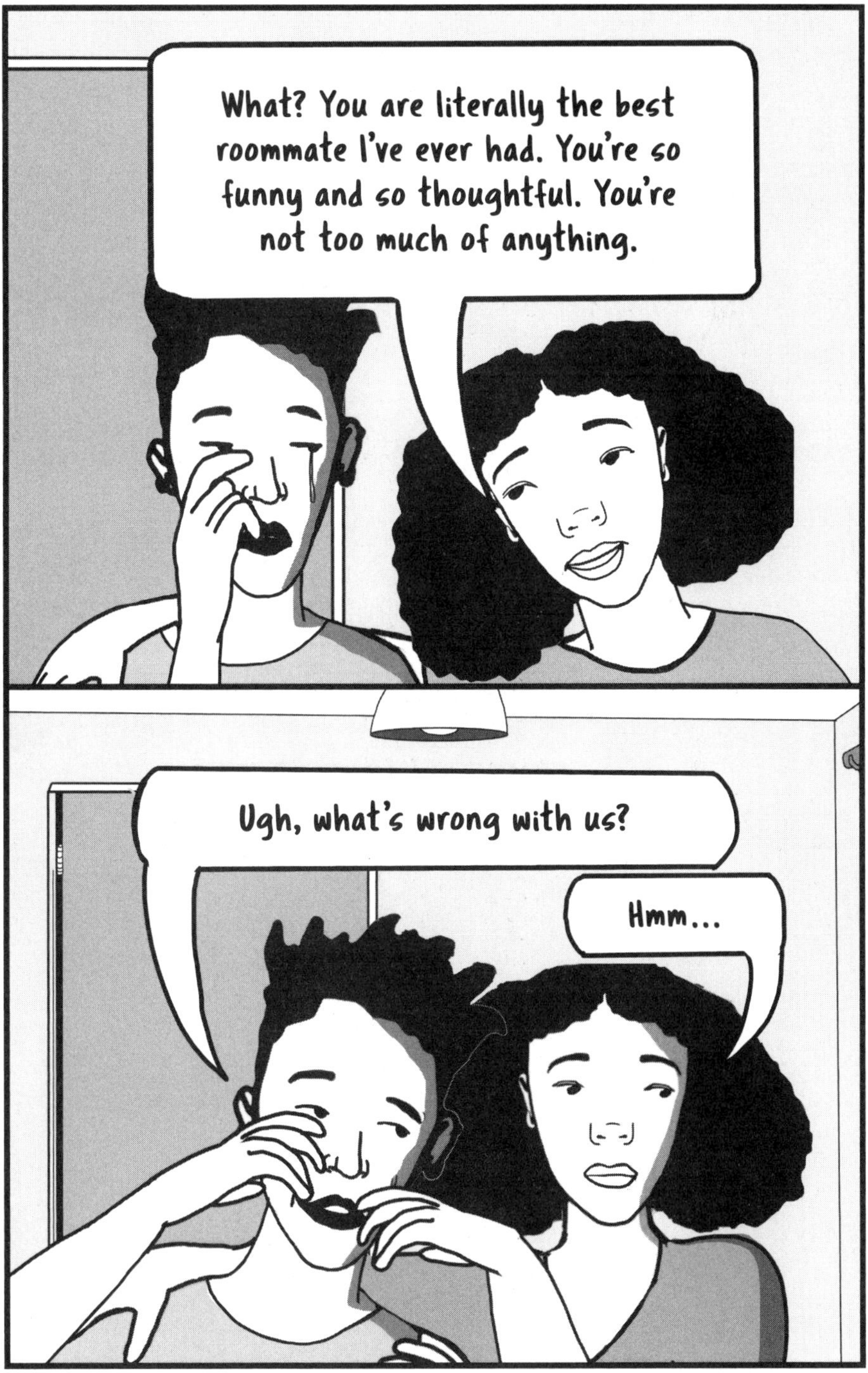
What? You are literally the best roommate I've ever had. You're so funny and so thoughtful. You're not too much of anything.
Ugh, what's wrong with us?
Hmm...

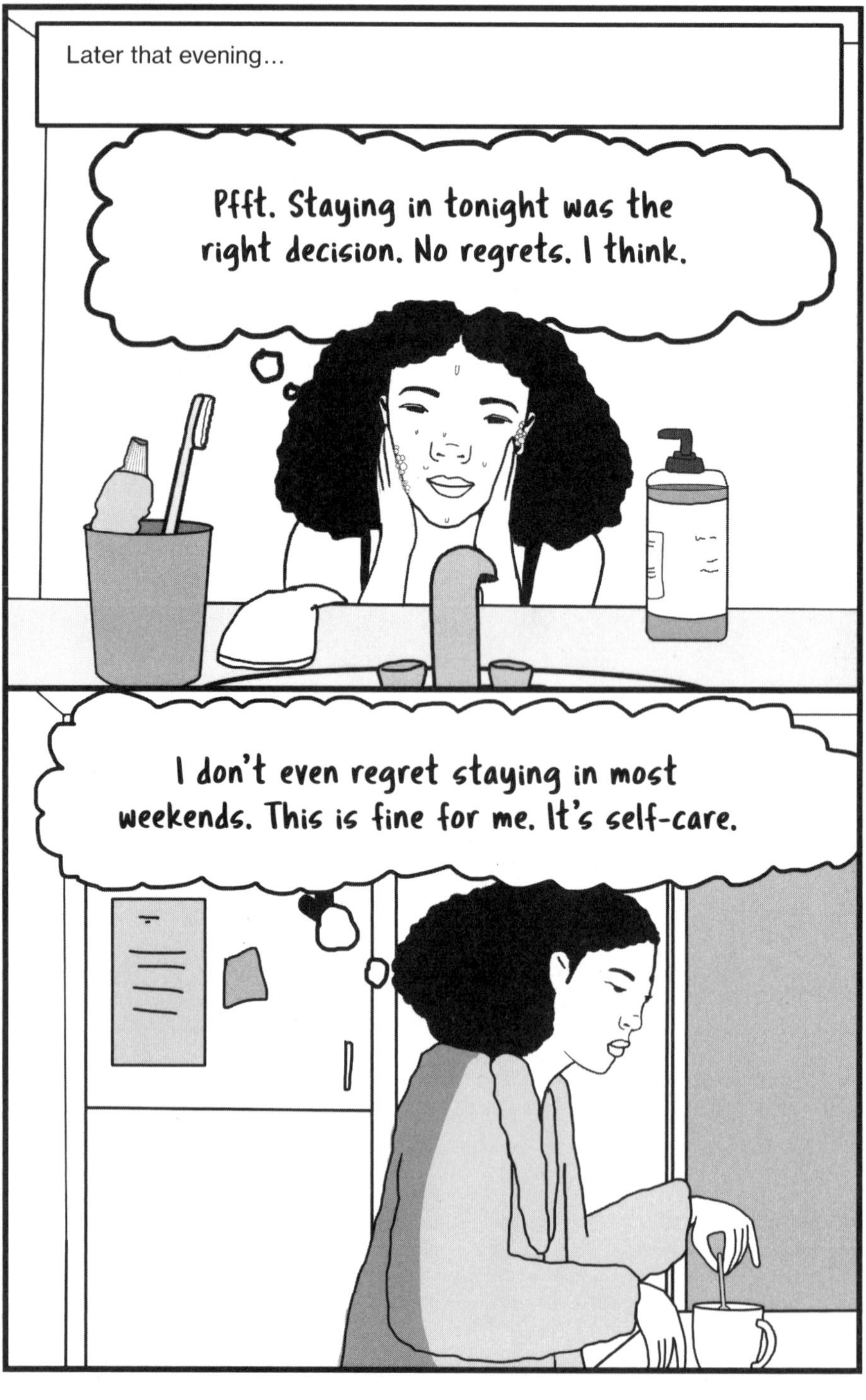
Later that evening...
Pfft. Staying in tonight was the right decision. No regrets. I think.
I don't even regret staying in most weekends. This is fine for me. It's self-care.

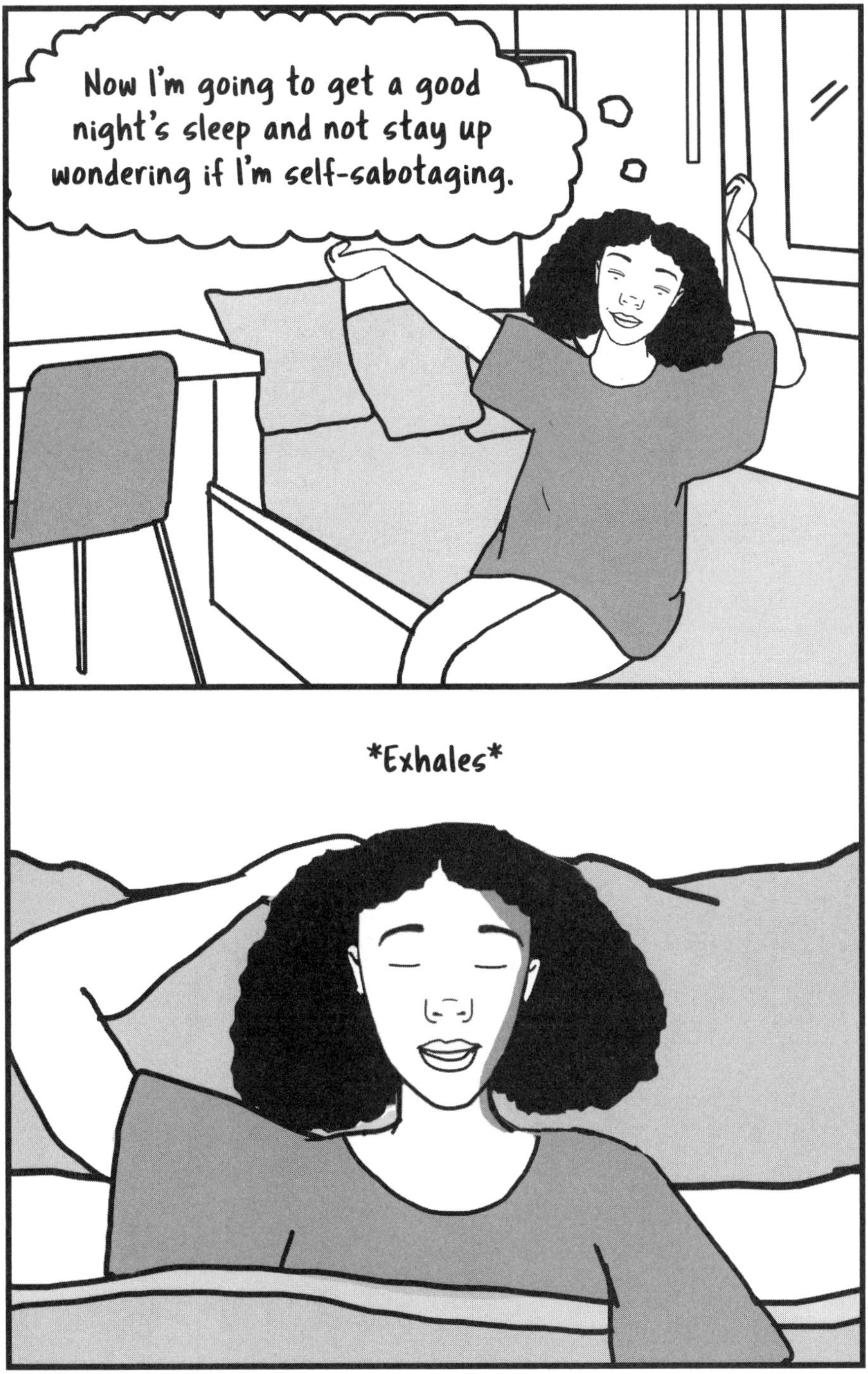
Now I'm going to get a good night's sleep and not stay up wondering if I'm self-sabotaging.
Exhales

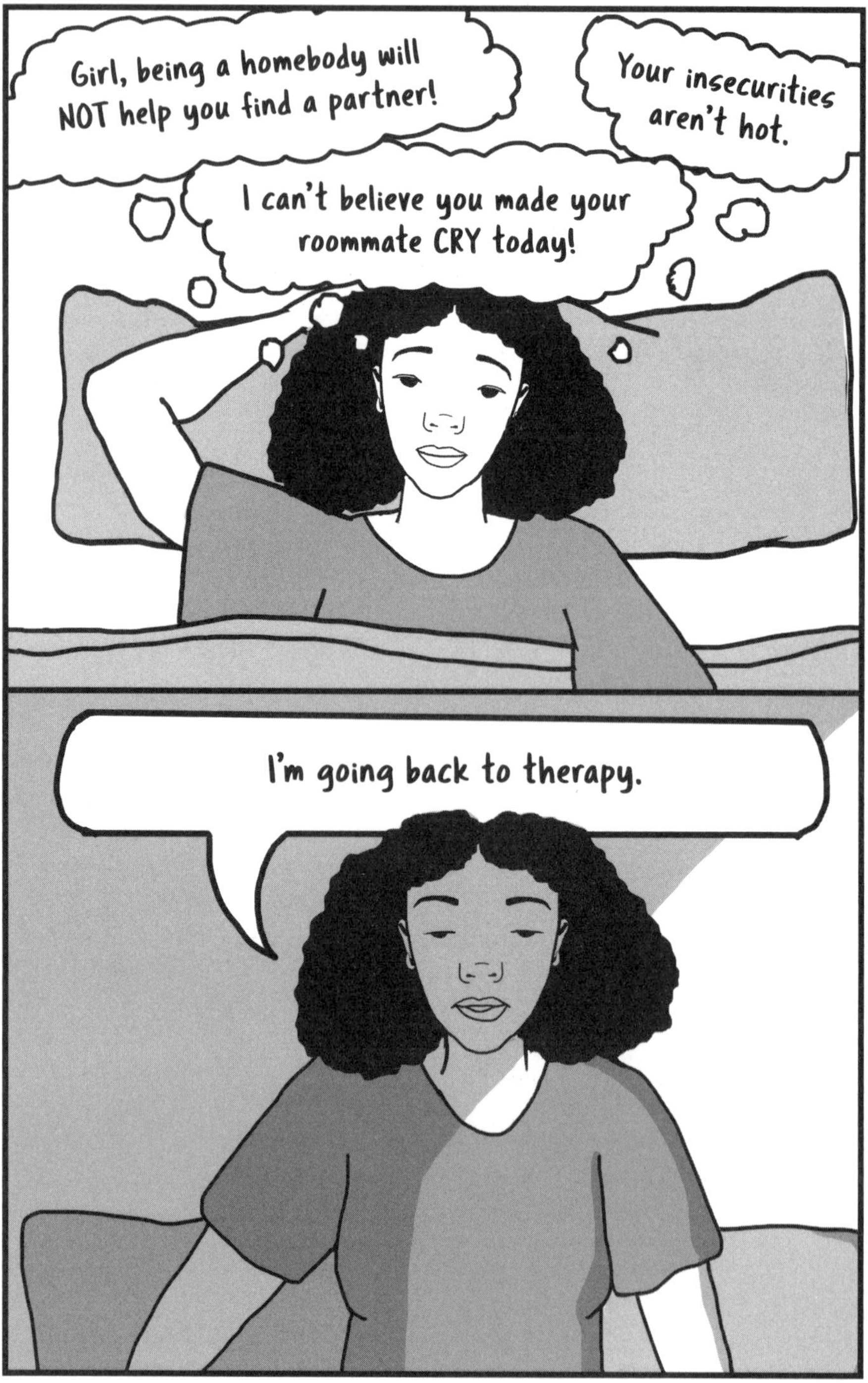
Girl, being a homebody will NOT help you find a partner!
Your insecurities aren't hot.
I can't believe you made your roommate CRY today!
I'm going back to therapy.

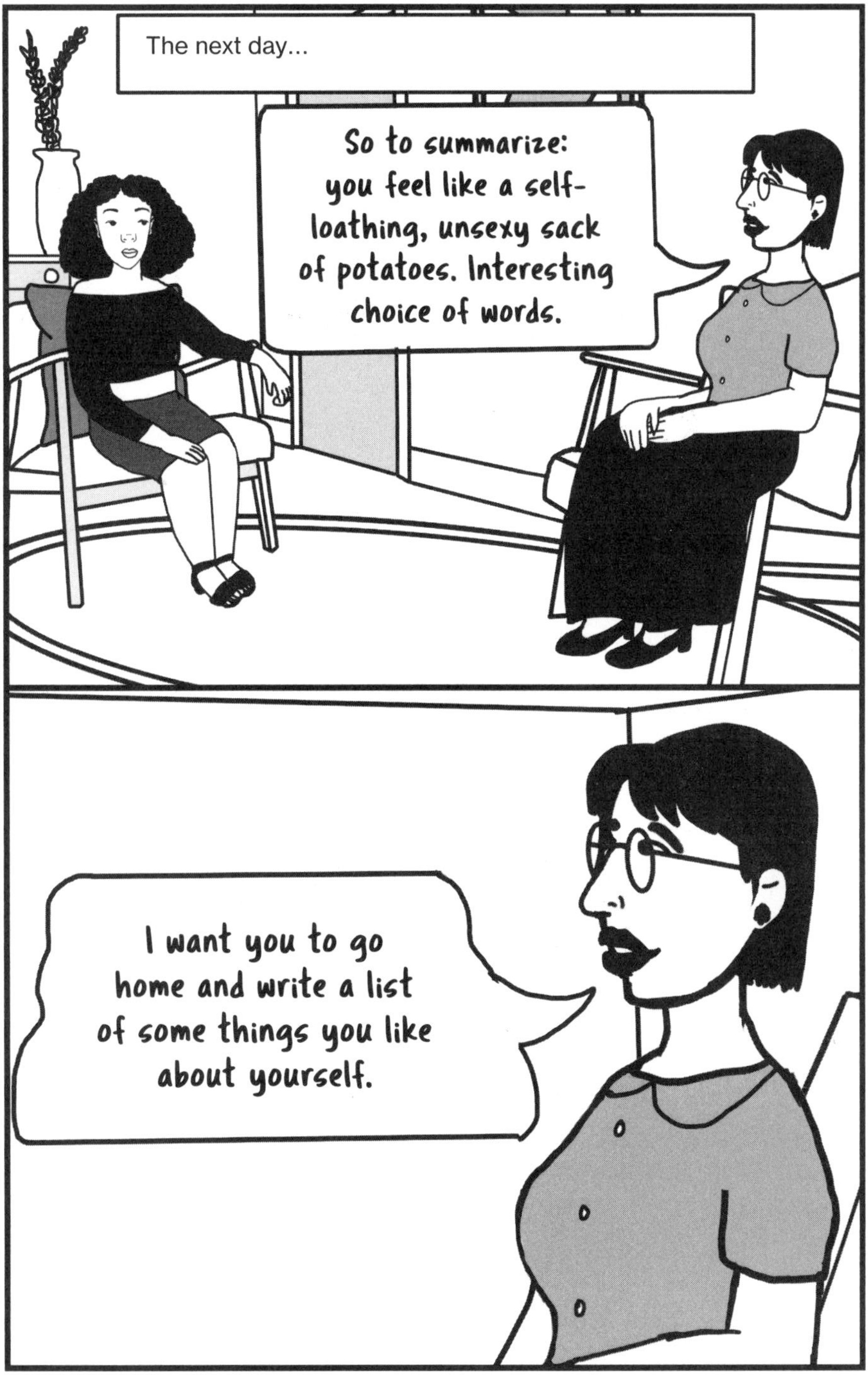
The next day...
So to summarize: you feel like a self-loathing, unsexy sack of potatoes. Interesting choice of words.
I want you to go home and write a list of some things you like about yourself.

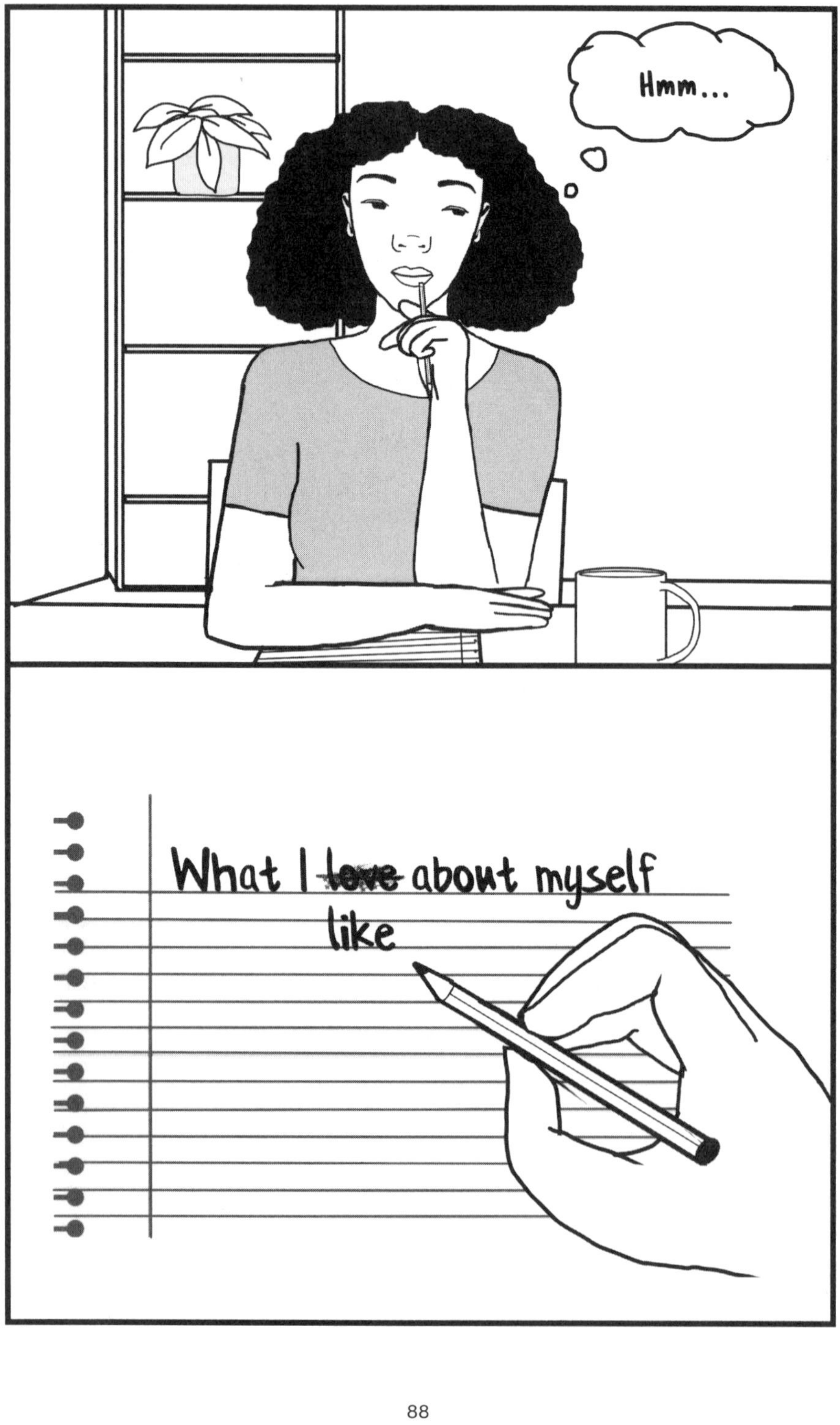
Hmm...
What I ~~love~~ about myself
like

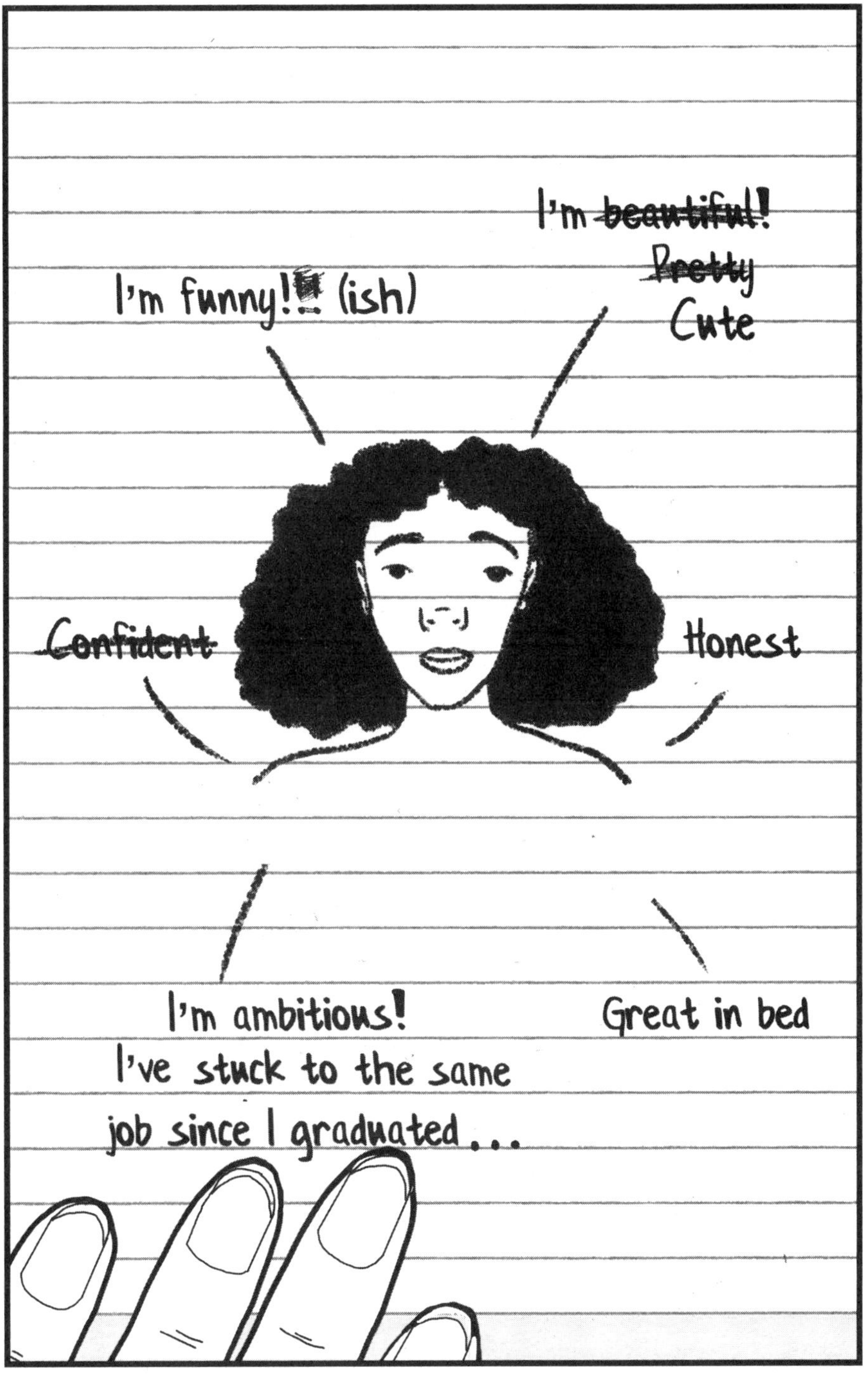

I'm ~~beautiful!~~
~~Pretty~~
Cute
I'm funny!~~!~~ (ish)
~~Confident~~
Honest
I'm ambitious!
I've stuck to the same
job since I graduated...
Great in bed

—

Stop waiting
for their text.
Go do some-
thing fun.

—

HOW TO TAKE YOURSELF ON A DATE

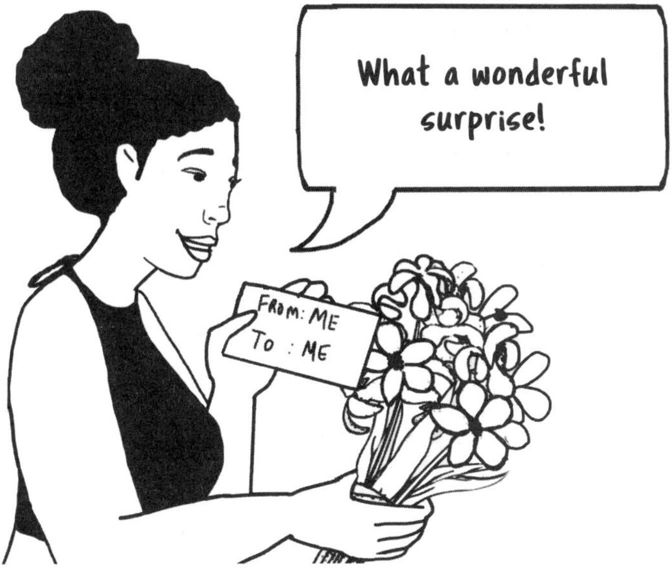

What a wonderful surprise!
FROM: ME
TO : ME

Step 1: Get Ready

A solo date is one to be taken just as seriously as a regular date. You should feel your best! Your evening could start with taking a warm bath or shower, exfoliating your skin, giving yourself a facial—whatever makes you feel good! Be sure your hygiene is at the same standard you would expect from a date. You deserve to look and feel good even on your own.

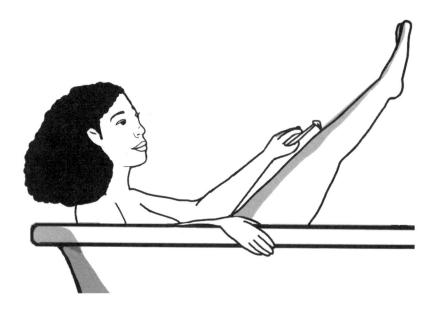

Step 2: Wear Something Cute

Again, emphasis on feeling *good.* This is not the same as heading to your local takeout place or café for a quick bite. Ditch the old T-shirt and joggers (unless they make you feel sexy!) and opt for something you feel beautiful in. Now is a better time than ever to wear that outfit you've been saving for a special occasion.

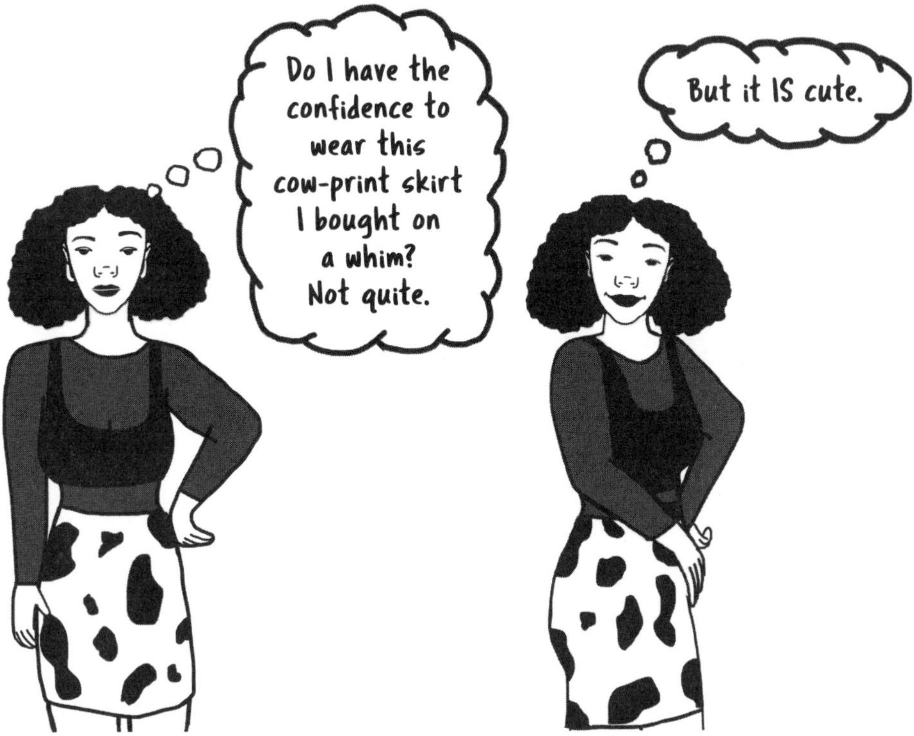
Do I have the confidence to wear this cow-print skirt I bought on a whim? Not quite.
But it IS cute.

Step 3: Plan an Activity

Okay, this is the challenging part. If you're not used to doing things on your own, planning fun solo activities might be way outside your comfort zone. However, the options are endless! You could visit a museum or art gallery, go to your favorite restaurant, watch a film, head to a rooftop bar, or have a picnic in the park. The best part is you get to choose and don't have to consider what anyone else wants to do.

Step 4: Give Yourself Compliments

Self-compliments are a great way to put pep in your step. Even if it feels too awkward to say it out loud, making the conscious effort to think positive thoughts about yourself is a sure way to feel loved and confident.

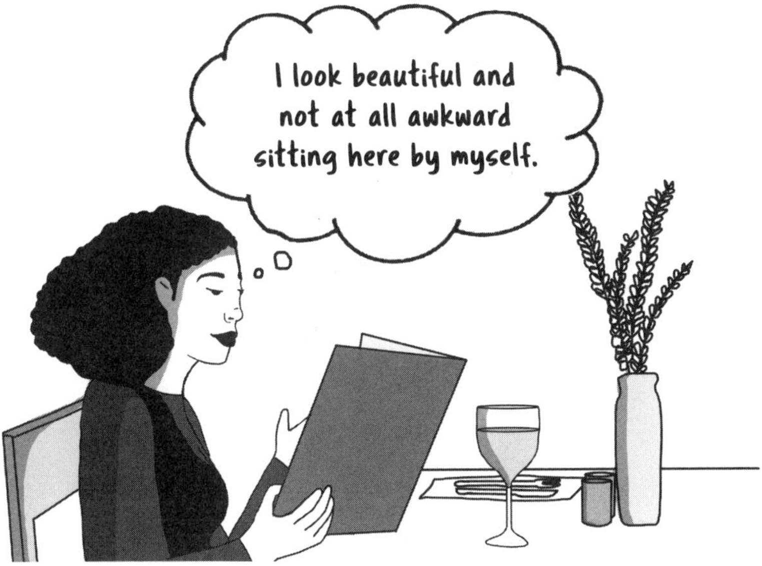
I look beautiful and not at all awkward sitting here by myself.

Step 5: Write Yourself a Love Letter

This activity is perfect if your date with yourself is at a restaurant or a place where you're seated alone. It is especially helpful if you aren't used to being alone or feel awkward being seen alone. Bring along something to write with so you can pen yourself a love letter—it is the epitome of personal romance. If it were socially acceptable to declare one's self-love out loud in public, that would be highly encouraged (honestly, go for it if that's your jam). Otherwise, simply writing a letter detailing all the reasons why you love you is the way to go.

Step 6: Thank Yourself

And that's a wrap. Once the date is over, you can thank yourself for the positive experience, however that looks for you. Hopefully you had a valuable experience that reminds you of what you expect from a date with a potential partner. Plus, it involves no awkward kiss or obligatory "Let's do this again sometime"!

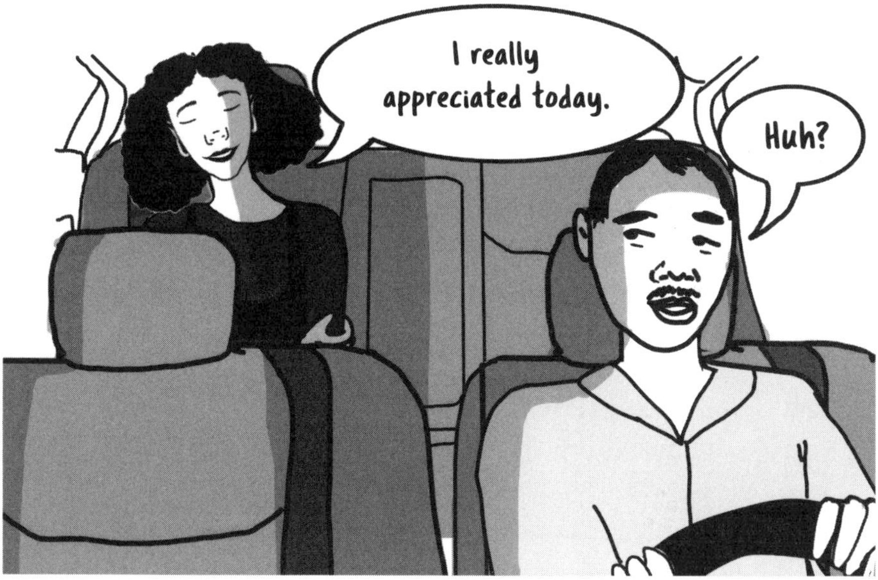
I really appreciated today.
Huh?

Creating Your *Own* Standards of Beauty

Practicing self-love can be an important step toward finding and building deep, intimate connection with another person, especially when you don't feel like you're on an equal playing field when dating. But self-love isn't a substitute for intimacy, and it's not always enough. For those of us from marginalized groups, dating doesn't always come as easily as it can for cis-het white people. For example, historically, women of color have felt pressure to adhere to white standards of beauty in the hopes of ever being deemed attractive. If our features are far from the European standards of beauty, it can be a daily struggle to muster up the self-esteem necessary to pursue a relationship. People with dark skin, fat bodies, wide noses, or coarse, curly hair, for example, are often overlooked in the dating world. Instead of being encouraged to address these prejudices, women of color are told—by dating experts, the media, and even family and friends—to love themselves first, which can feel dismissive. Doing internal work toward self-love and acceptance is important, but it can only get you so far when it comes to pursuing romance. Changing the culture's definition of beauty, as reflected in movies and TV and other media, would be a big step toward addressing this serious challenge in the dating world.

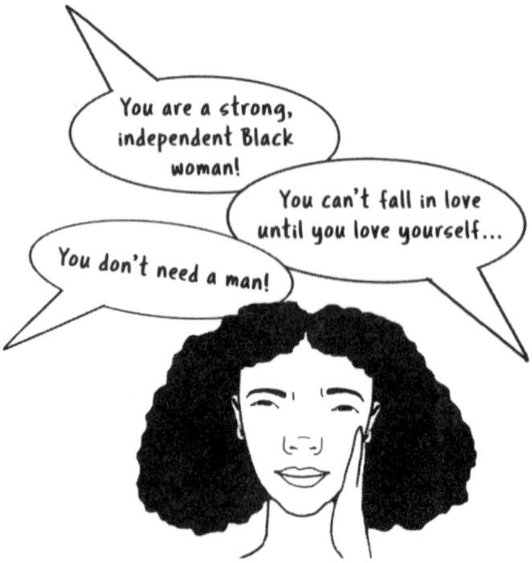
You are a strong, independent Black woman!
You can't fall in love until you love yourself...
You don't need a man!

In the meantime, how do we as people of marginalized groups find a balance between accepting that dating is hard and pursuing love anyway? Wanting to be in a relationship is a natural and valid desire. It's in no way your fault that some people came along and convinced the world that there's only one way to be beautiful. Everyone has an equal right to be loved and doted on. Part of self-love is regularly reminding yourself that

you are deserving of love from both internal and external sources. If humans were meant to solely rely on themselves for love and intimacy, none of us would be here.

As tough as it may be at times, we must gently nurse the parts of ourselves that don't meet our society's standards of beauty. For dark-skinned people, that could involve educating yourself on the roots of colorism, following more people on social media with your skin tone, or wearing bright, bold colors that bring out your complexion. For fat people, this could be unfollowing content on social media that makes you feel bad about your appearance, empowering yourself to challenge internalized fat phobia, or celebrating your body by wearing literally whatever you want! This is all a part of dating yourself—radically accepting yourself without conditions and knowing that there's far more to you than your physical appearance. You wouldn't date someone who says, "You'd be way hotter if your skin was just a bit lighter," so why on earth would you say something like that to yourself?

Your relationship with yourself isn't linear. It's long, strange, fraught, and remarkable and can lead you to deep insights. What we learn about ourselves along the way informs our selection process when it comes to a potential partner. When you know what you deserve and that you're capable of giving yourself those very things, it's hard to settle for less. It's not really about what you bring to the table, but *who*.

CHAPTER FIVE

YOU WON'T MEET THEM BY WAITING

FUTURE HUSBAND
KNOCK THRICE!

You Won't Meet Them by Waiting

When it comes to dating, at some point, actively putting yourself out there is unavoidable. This can be daunting, no matter who you are. The idea of going out and meeting a stranger, in person, can be especially intimidating for those of us who have grown up in a digital age, when our love life often begins within dating apps on a device. It's easy to feel overwhelmed by the options, of having thousands of faces to swipe through on a screen—and by the fact that we appear as one face among thousands ourselves. As we've learned from the previous chapters, to get the most out of dating, it makes a world of difference to start your search with a positive mindset, good self-esteem, and a clear picture of what you want in a partner. Once you're on your way with those steps, it is time to start weaving your love life into your best life, approaching meeting new people with an open heart.

Whether finding the right person is a matter of sheer luck or—just like anything you want in life—dependent on strategy and consistency is up for debate. As mentioned in the previous chapter, there are many factors that might hinder a person's ability to find a partner. But if you know dating is something you really want and yet struggle to put into practice, it might be time to investigate why and take some proactive, concrete steps toward meeting new people.

Dating apps are one way to get the ball rolling. Let's face it, for many people, matching on an app is a lot easier than walking up to someone in a bar or waiting to be approached—you can date from wherever you are, whenever you want. On the flip side, it can hinder one's ability to make deeper connections. Do you avoid chatting with people once you've made a match? Are you having prolonged conversations in the app but shying away from meeting in person?

Swipe!

Swipe!

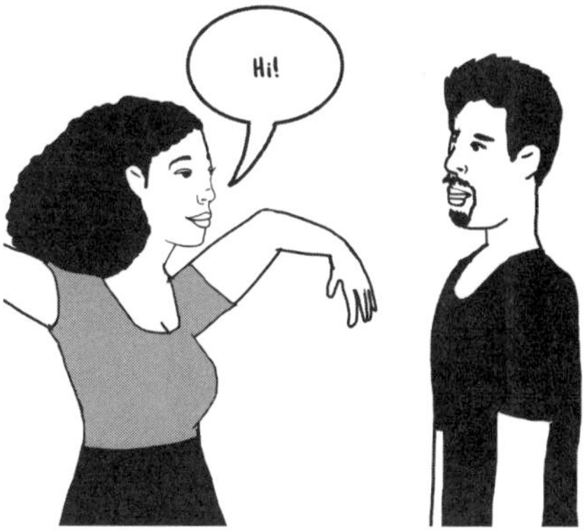
Hi!

To get the most out of dating apps, it's important to create a profile that highlights some of your best qualities. The first of those qualities is, of course, your physical appearance. It's time to scrap the selfie you took years ago in a poorly lit room when your hair or sense of style was totally different from what it is now. Opt for a recent picture that shows your matches what you look like in this stage of your life. Choose other photos that highlight positive aspects of your life: favorite hobbies, activities with friends and family, traveling. In addition, ensure your bio and prompts are fun and inviting. Words and phrases that identify you as friendly, approachable, and personable can spark conversation. Knowing that your match is a seemingly normal person makes online dating feel safer for everyone.

Once your matches know what you look like, it's time to showcase your personality through the magic of writing. Keep your bio open, friendly, and inviting. Highlight your interests— travel, cooking, sci-fi movies, animals, for example. It's okay to be honest about what you're seeking in a partner. Remember that being specific is more likely to connect you to who you're looking for and help weed out people you're not compatible with. Avoid writing long lists about what you're *not* looking for. Focusing on the kind of person you'd like to match with is a much more productive way to make use of dating apps.

If dating apps are not your thing, meeting someone the old-fashioned way, IRL, is always an option. For some people, though, the thought of approaching a stranger they find attractive fills them with crippling anxiety. What do you say? How close do you stand? What the hell do you do with your hands? It doesn't have to be like a movie or TV show where the cis-het woman conveniently sits down at a bar next to the most gorgeous cis-het man on earth who just happens to have been watching her all night and *obviously* decides to start a conversation. It does, however, require you to take a few pages from her book and actually go out and strategically place yourself where the kind of people you like generally hang out.

By indulging in the act of dating yourself, you will start to get a sense of the kinds of places you feel comfortable spending time. If you don't yet know, this is where the fun begins! If, for example, you're really into music, going to local concerts, clubs, or jam sessions—or looking out for meet-ups and social media groups of people with similar music tastes—could be great ways to meet new people. If the anxiety of going alone is holding you back, bring some friends to make it easier to strike up conversation with new people. You could even ask a friend to start the conversation and introduce you to people you're interested in. Even if you don't exchange numbers, making a new connection with someone is a good confidence booster for when you try again next time.

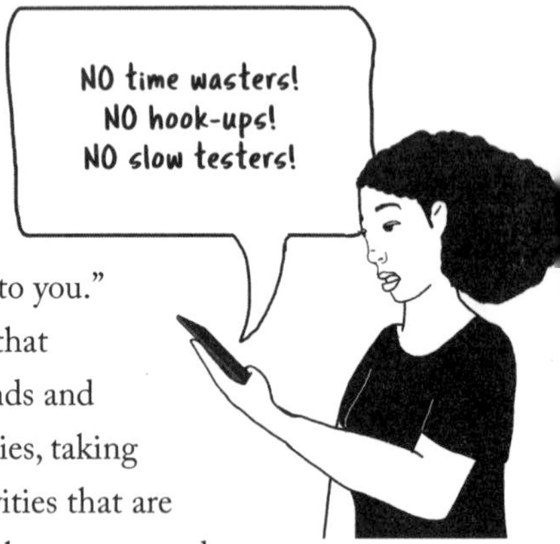
NO time wasters!
NO hook-ups!
NO slow testers!

Being adventurous, going out into the world, and doing things that you enjoy makes you more likely to meet other people. We've all heard the saying "You find love when you stop looking," but maybe it's more along the lines of "You find love when you act like it's available to you." That means that while you're busy doing things that make you happy—spending time with your friends and family, focusing on your job, pursuing your hobbies, taking care of your physical self, or whatever other activities that are important to you—you're already creating a life that accommodates the kind of romance you're looking for.

A note on making the first move: if you're going out to intentionally meet someone you want to date, it's important to find settings where it's appropriate to flirt with strangers and establish consent for doing so. Many of us are not really in the habit of talking to strangers at all, especially if you're not a cis-het man. For one, that's not always a safe or appropriate option, and understanding other people's intentions and boundaries is an essential part of flirting. But there are also social norms around men as the pursuers and women as the pursued, an objectifying and disempowering notion that prevents women from going after what they want—and that doesn't translate very well in non-cis-het relationships. As attitudes around gender roles continue to become more flexible, we are learning, as a culture, how limiting these attitudes can be, and creating new norms. Sometimes there is no norm! You can try out whatever approach feels comfortable and see what feels right for you. Maybe you enjoy or benefit from the dynamics of being approached by someone else first. Maybe you like making the first move. When you're finally in the driver's seat of your love life, it becomes clearer that it's totally up to you.

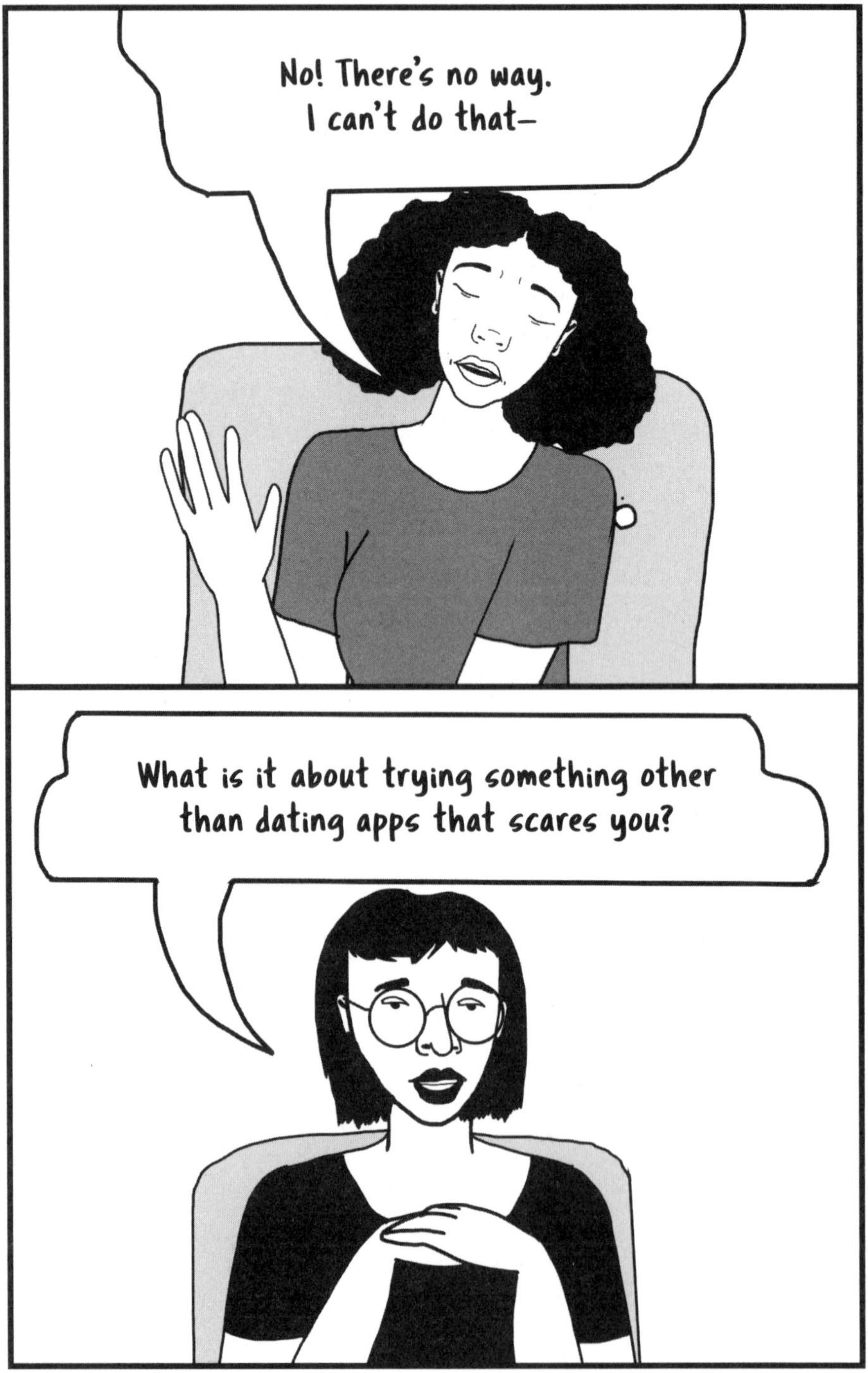
No! There's no way.
I can't do that–
What is it about trying something other than dating apps that scares you?

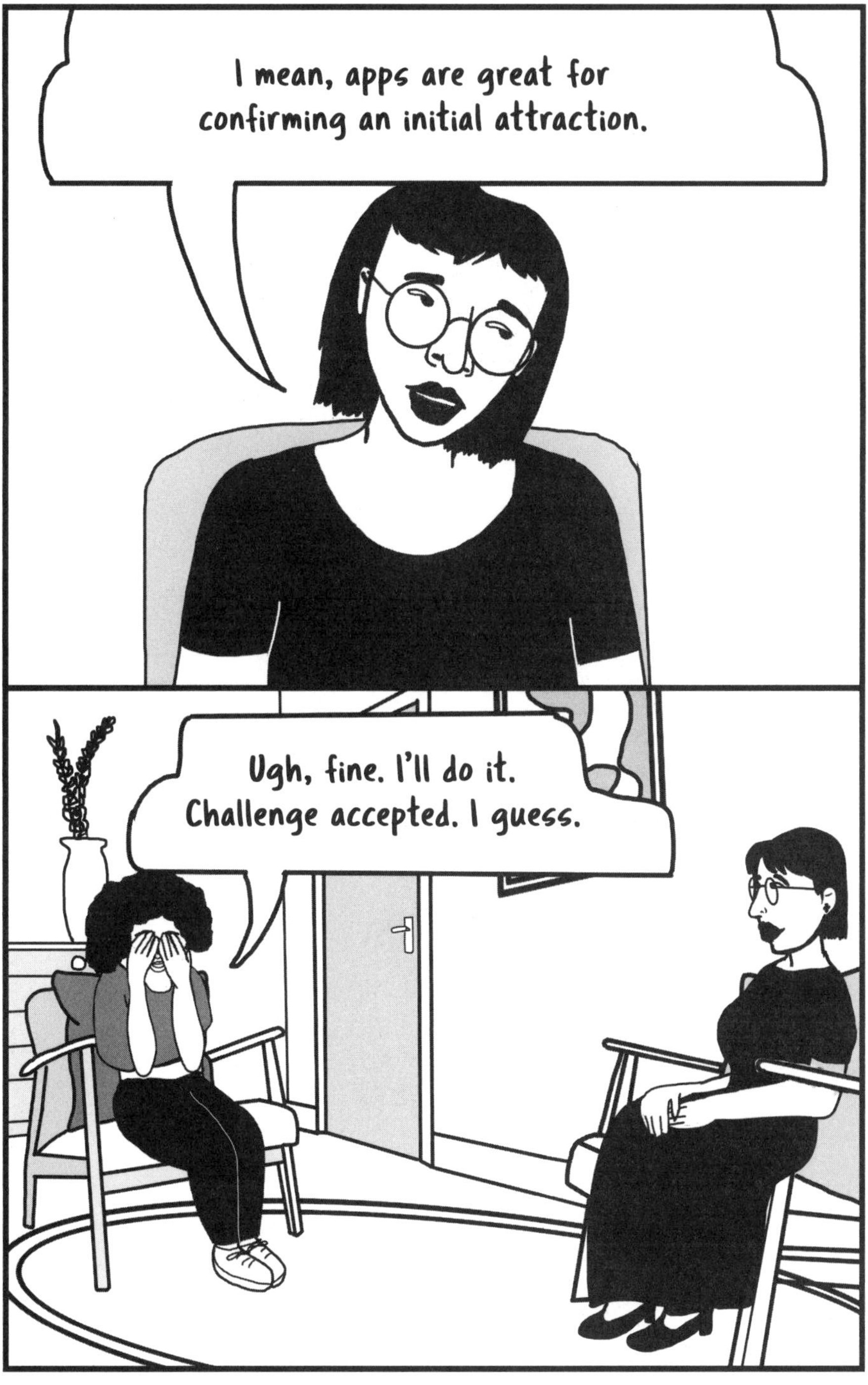
I mean, apps are great for confirming an initial attraction.
Ugh, fine. I'll do it. Challenge accepted. I guess.

Challenge 1:
Talk to That Hot Guy at the Farmers' Market

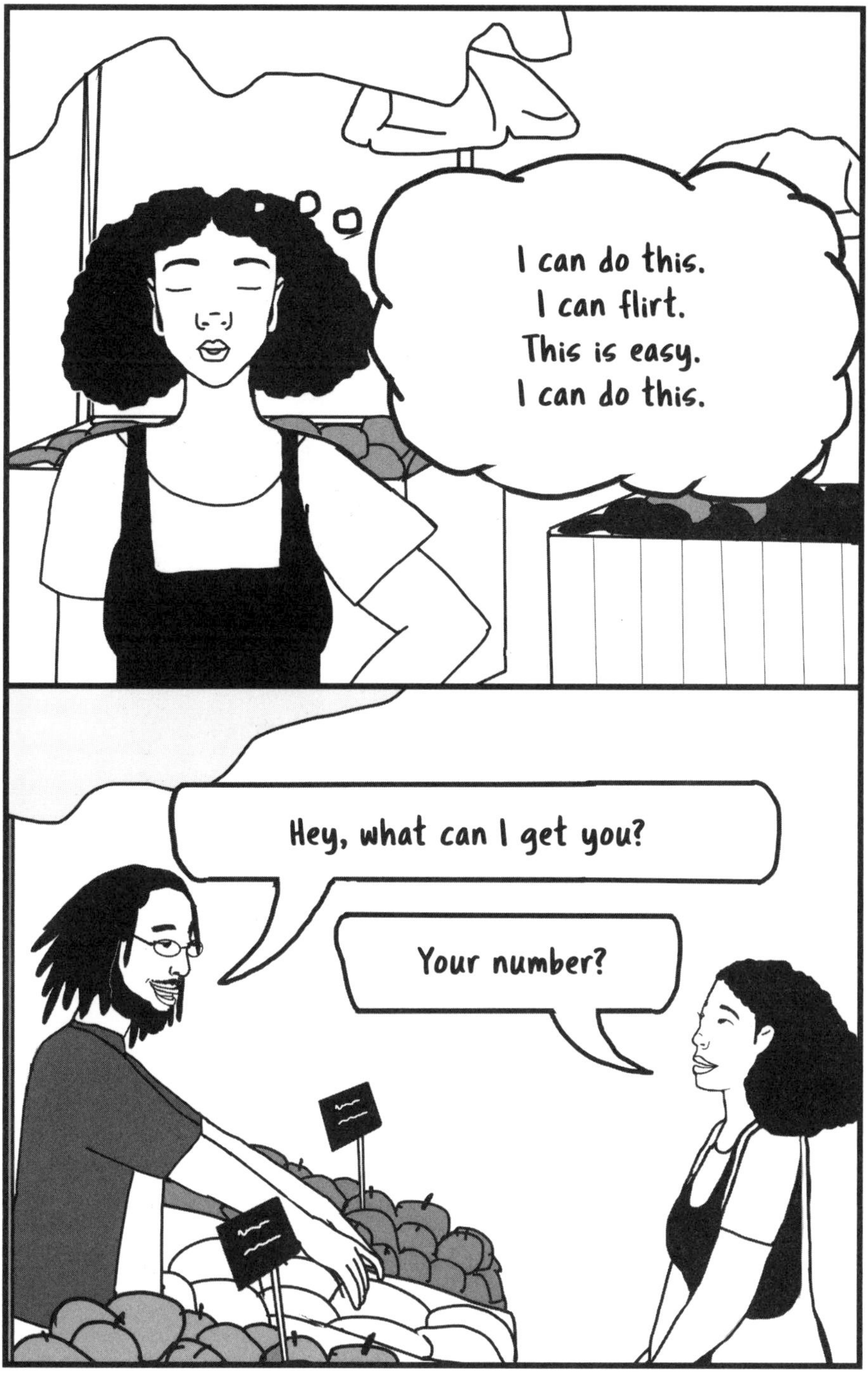
I can do this.
I can flirt.
This is easy.
I can do this.
Hey, what can I get you?
Your number?

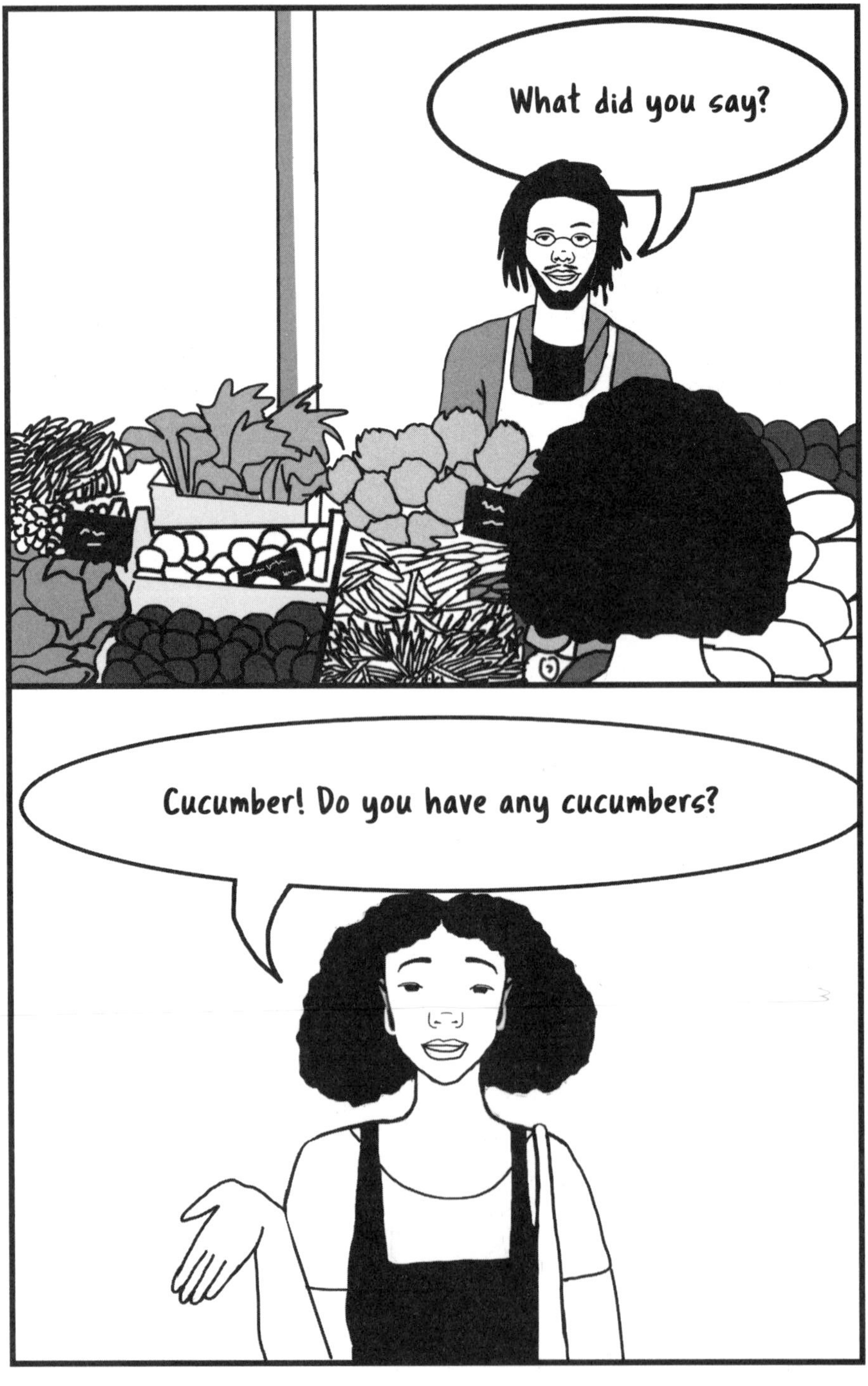
What did you say?
Cucumber! Do you have any cucumbers?

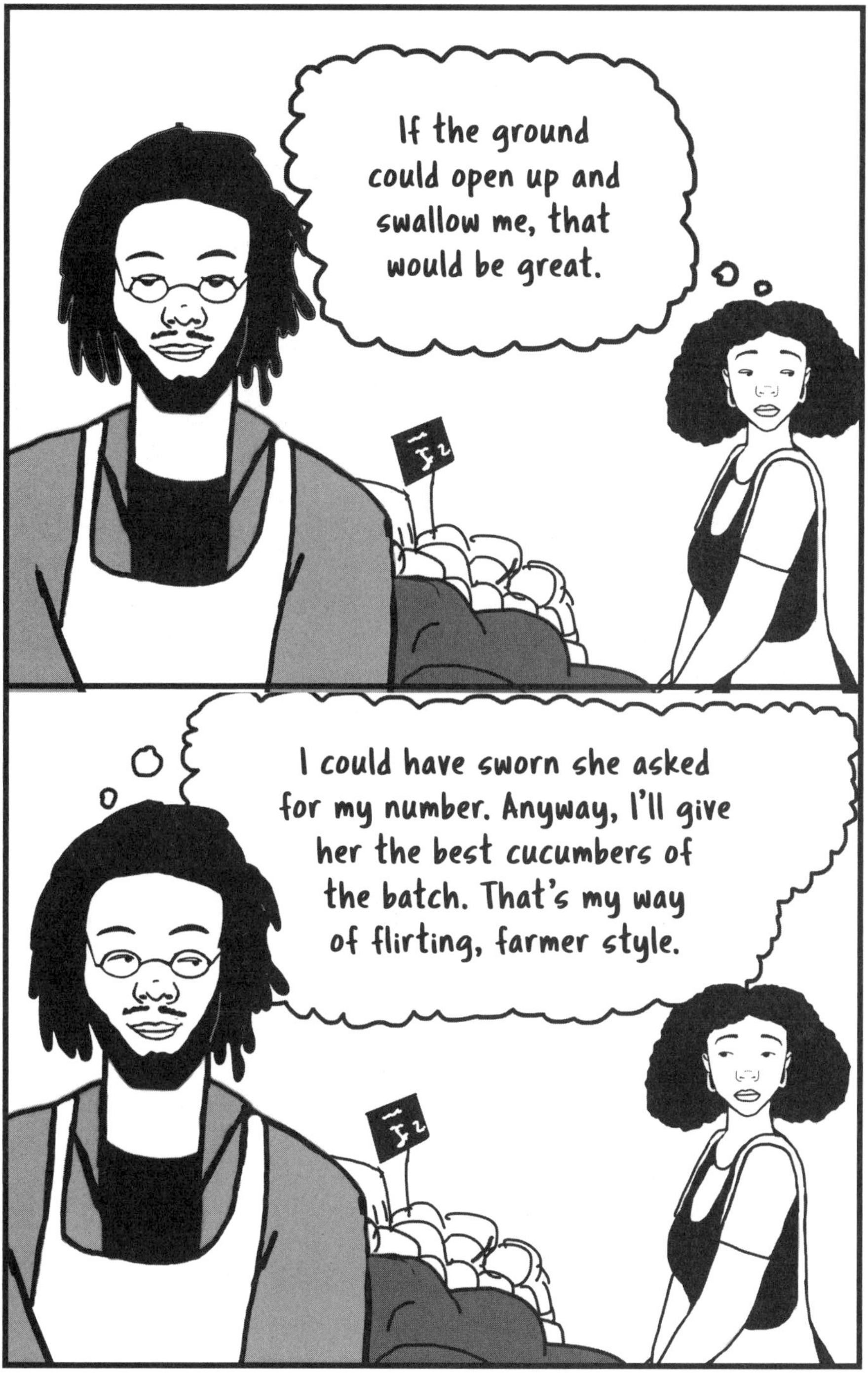
If the ground could open up and swallow me, that would be great.
I could have sworn she asked for my number. Anyway, I'll give her the best cucumbers of the batch. That's my way of flirting, farmer style.

Challenge 2:
Blind Date

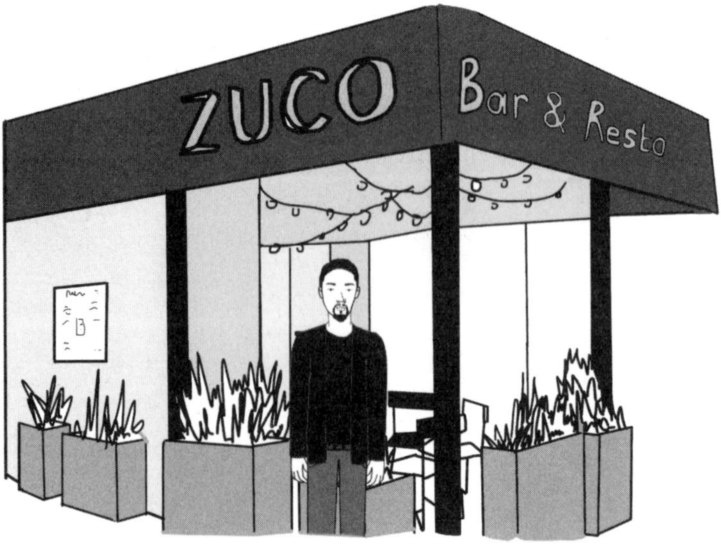
ZUCO
Bar & Resto

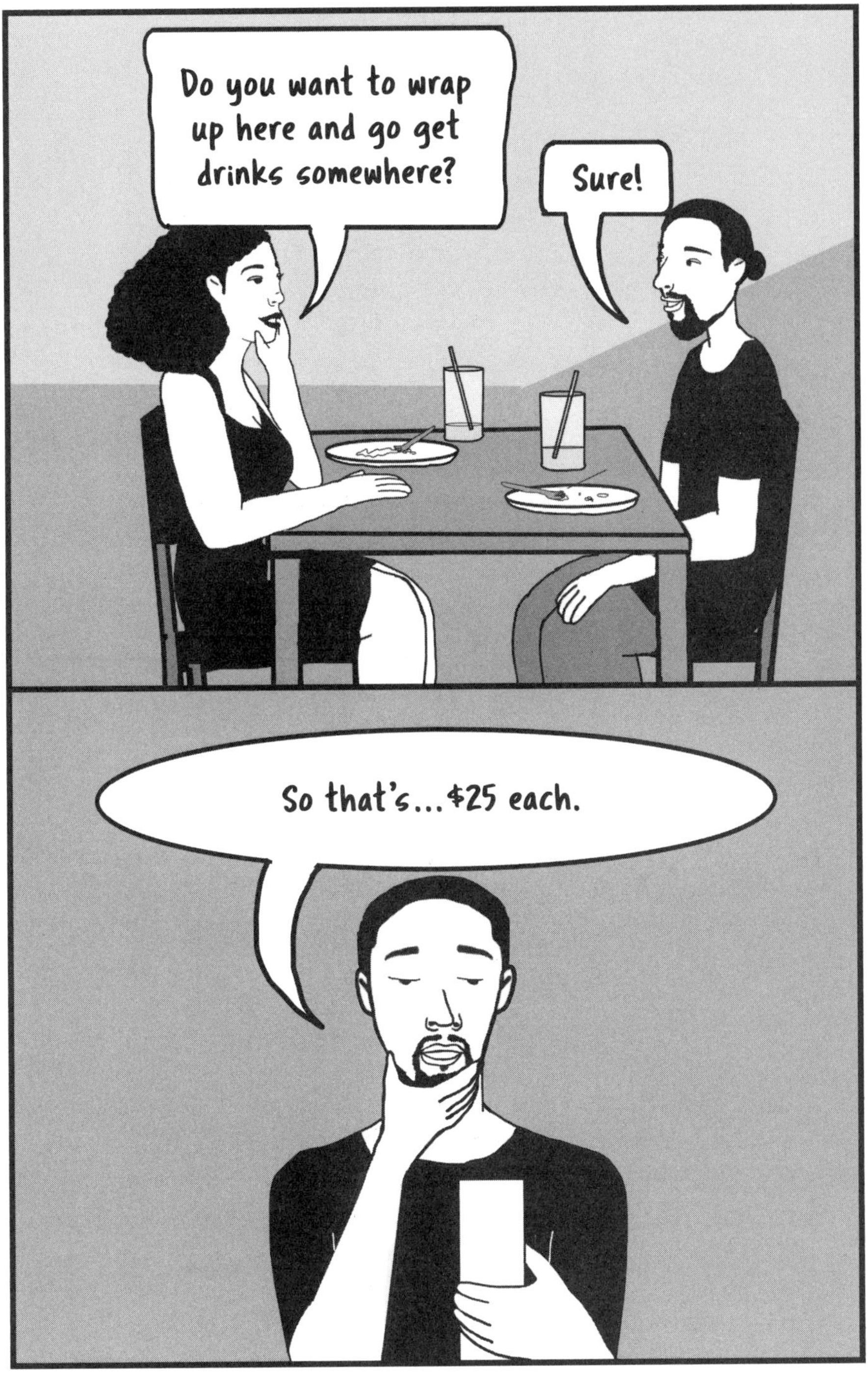
Do you want to wrap up here and go get drinks somewhere?
Sure!
So that's... $25 each.

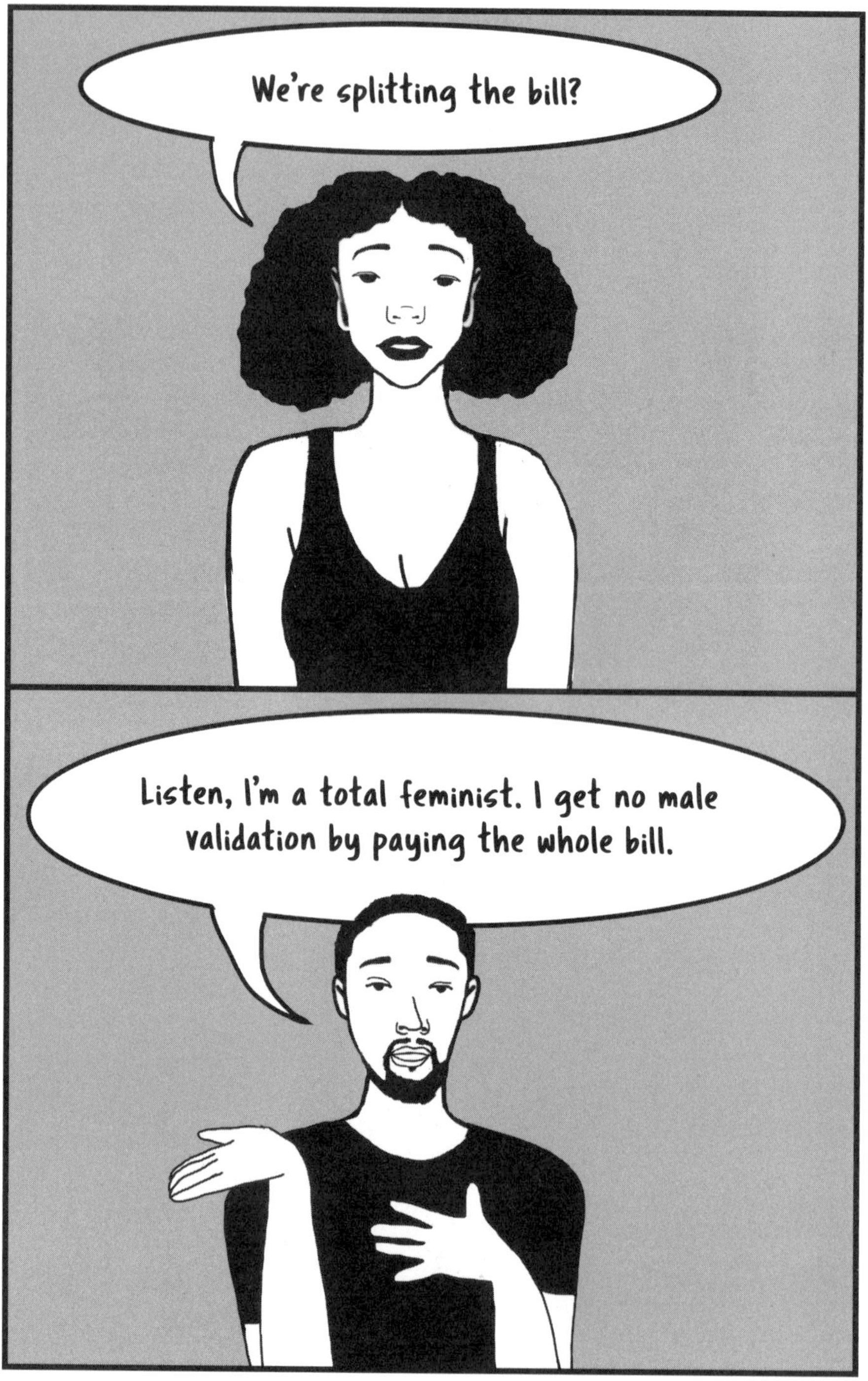
We're splitting the bill?
Listen, I'm a total feminist. I get no male validation by paying the whole bill.

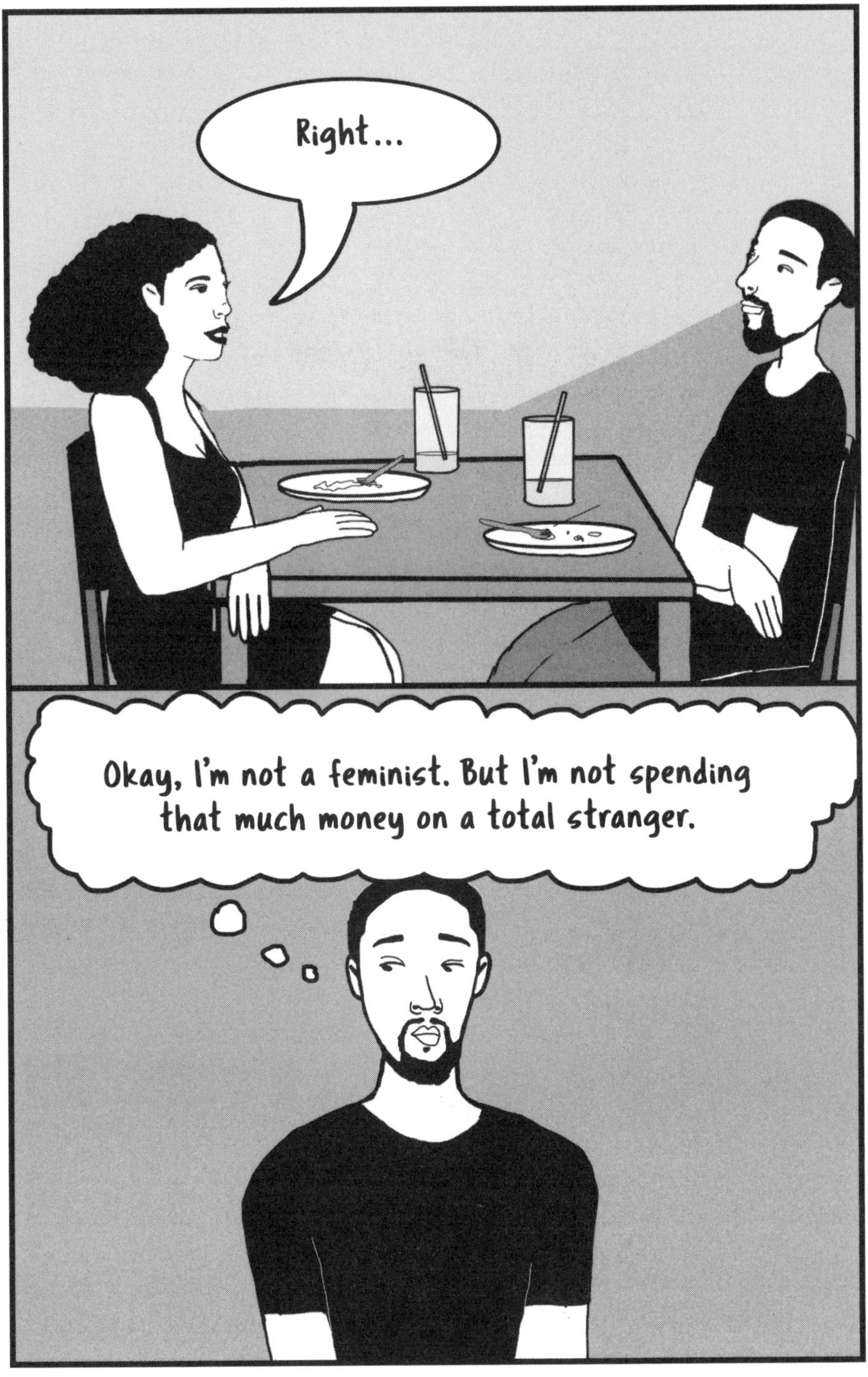
Right...
Okay, I'm not a feminist. But I'm not spending that much money on a total stranger.

Challenge 3:
Rekindle an Old Flame

●●●○○ EE 4G
23:00
75%
Messages
Trash Ex
Details
Hey big head
Hey
Text Message

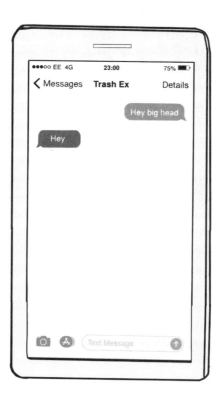

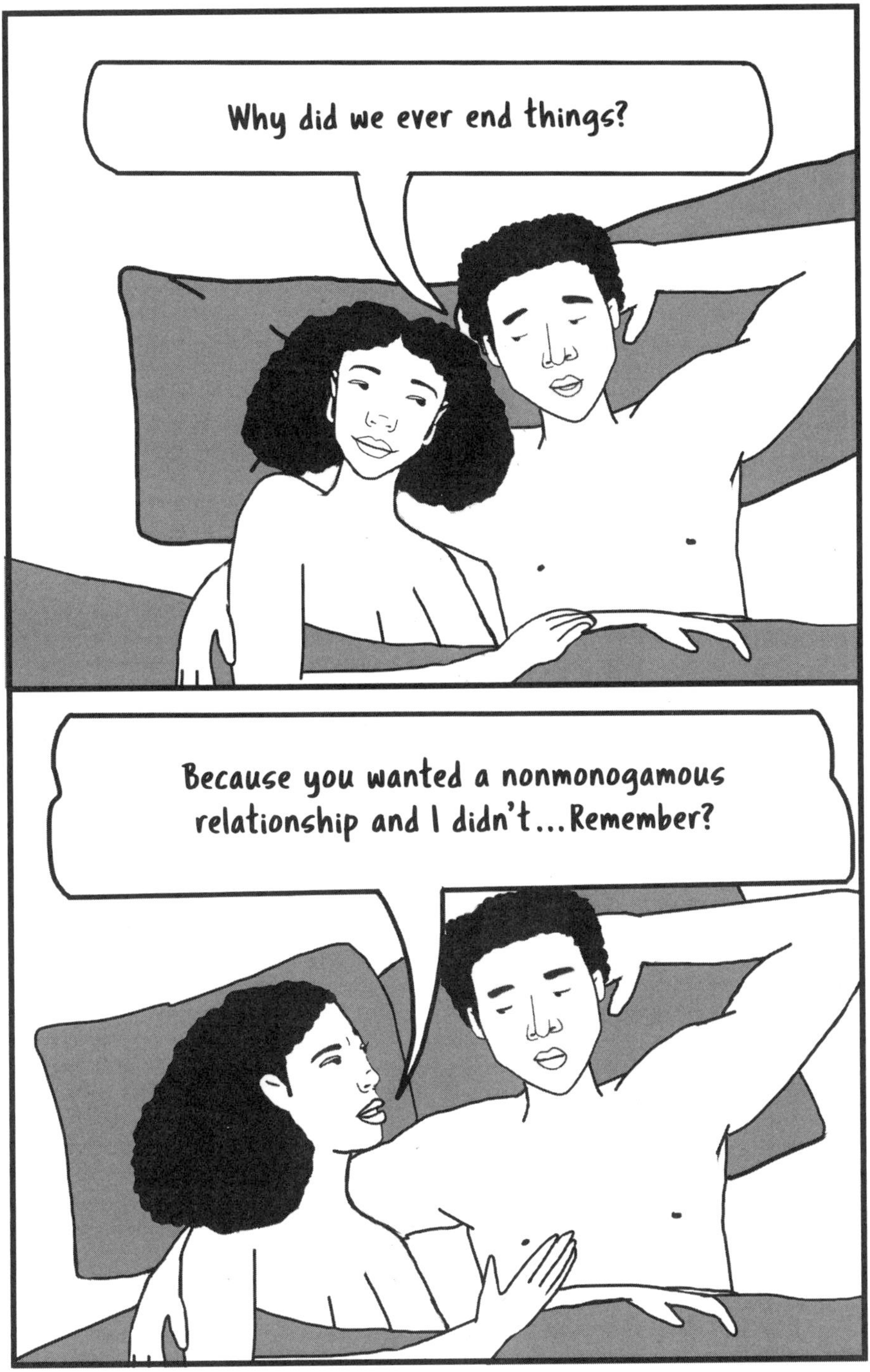
Why did we ever end things?
Because you wanted a nonmonogamous relationship and I didn't...Remember?

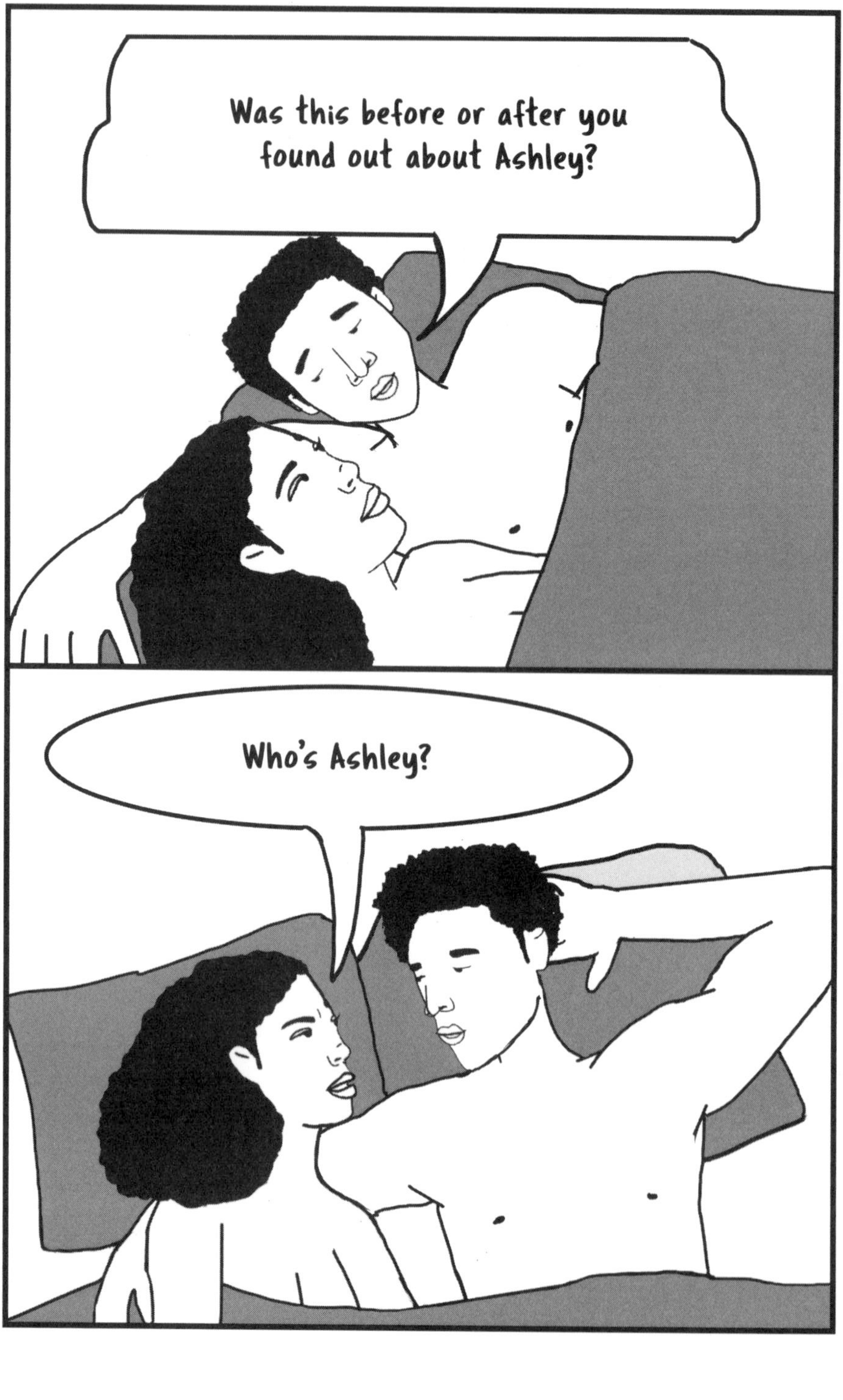
Was this before or after you found out about Ashley?
Who's Ashley?

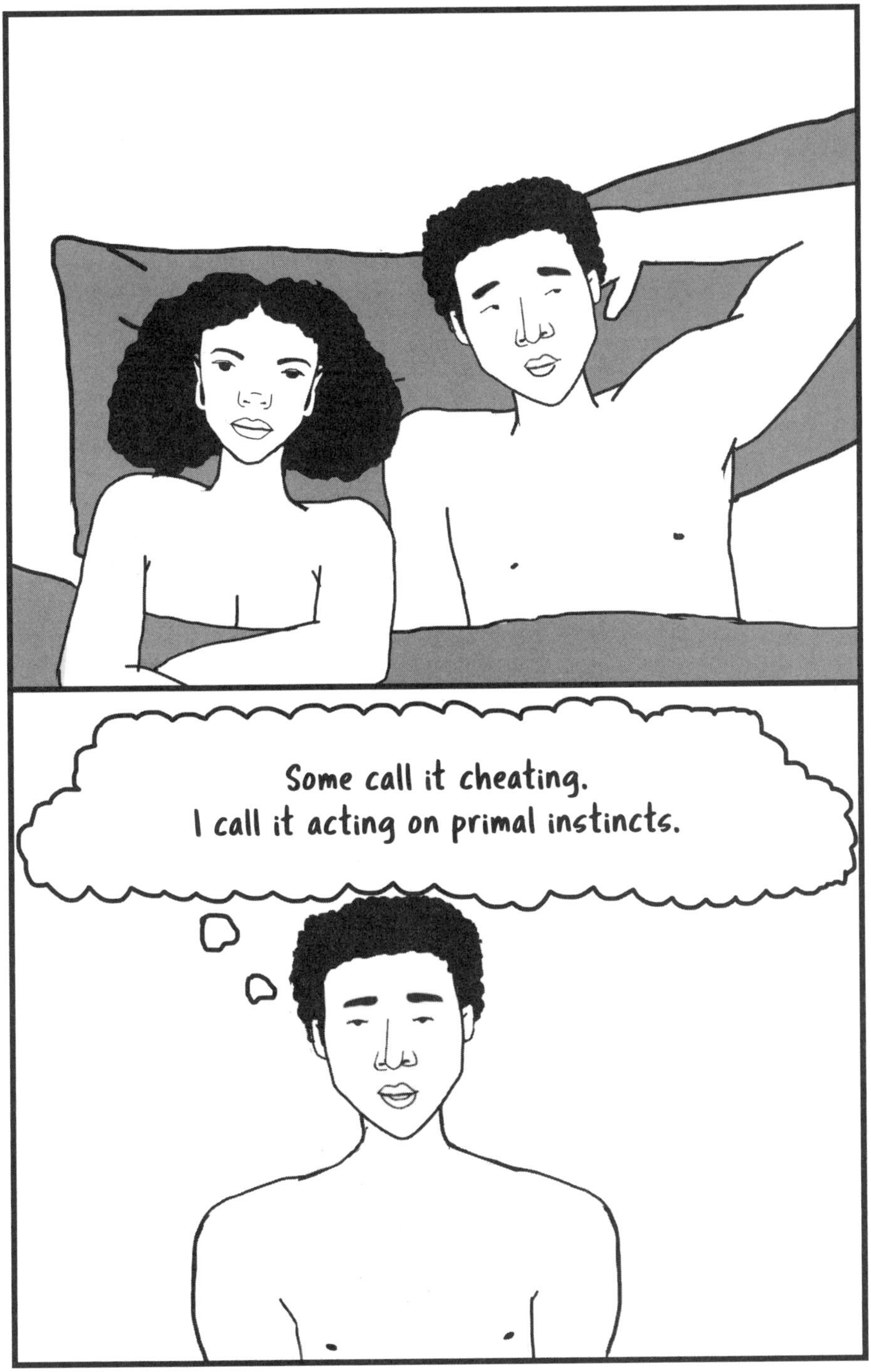
Some call it cheating.
I call it acting on primal instincts.

Challenge 4:
Gather Some Wingwomen

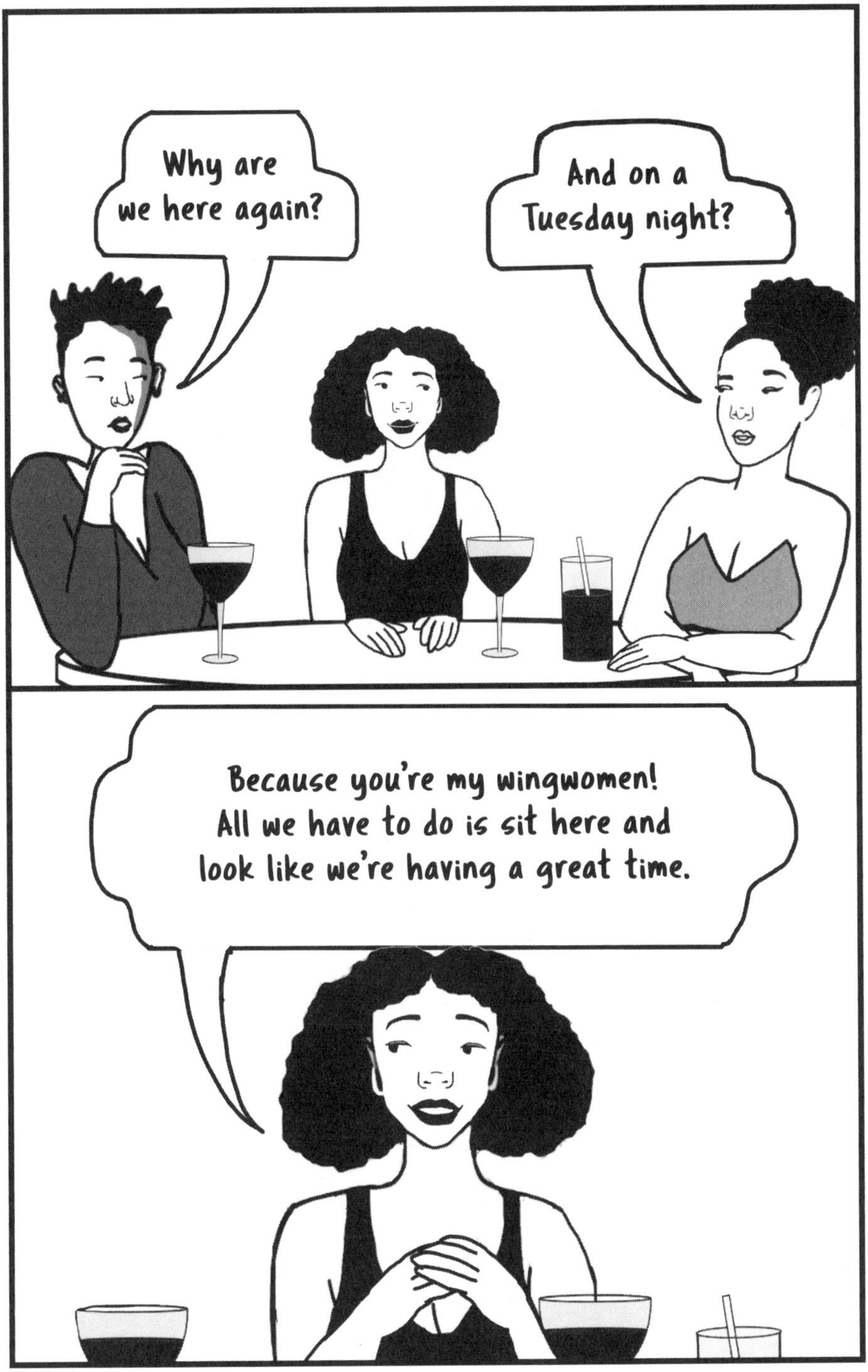
Why are we here again?
And on a Tuesday night?
Because you're my wingwomen! All we have to do is sit here and look like we're having a great time.

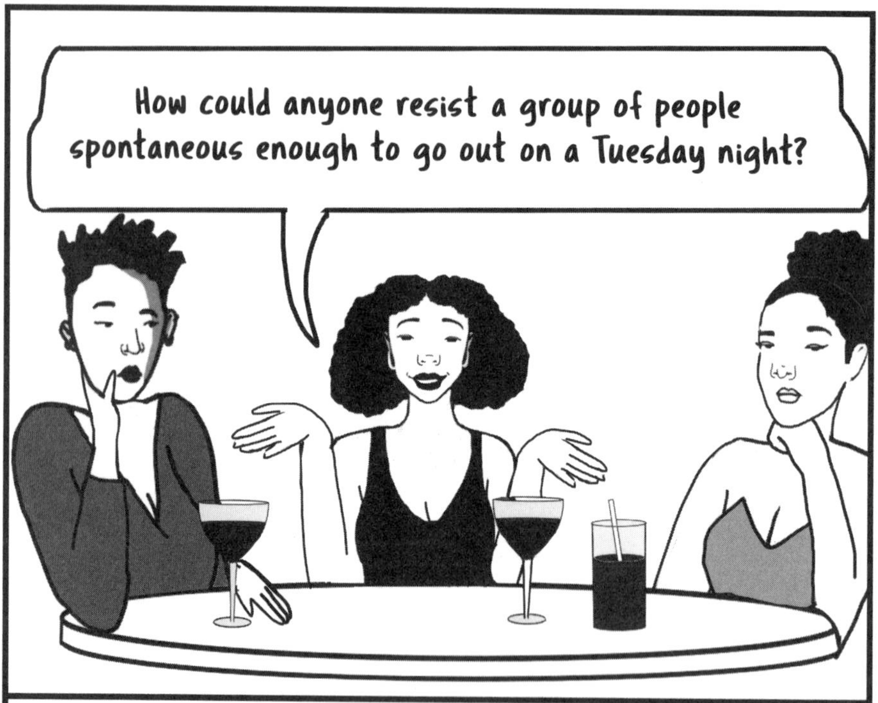
How could anyone resist a group of people spontaneous enough to go out on a Tuesday night?

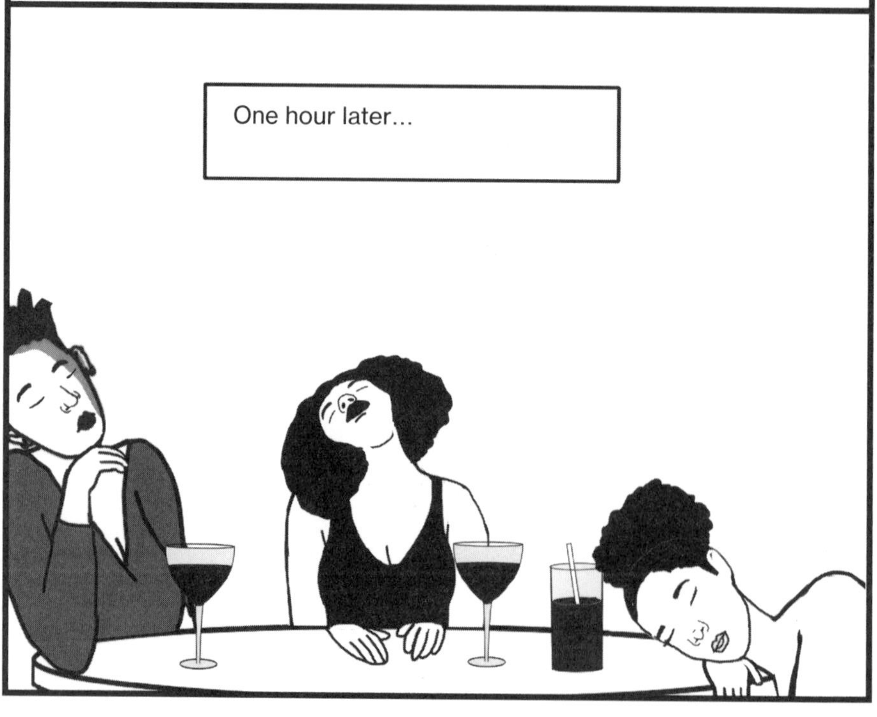
One hour later...

—

You're allowed
to change
your mind
about the people
you date.

—

CHAPTER SIX

HOW TO KNOW YOU'VE FOUND THE ONE

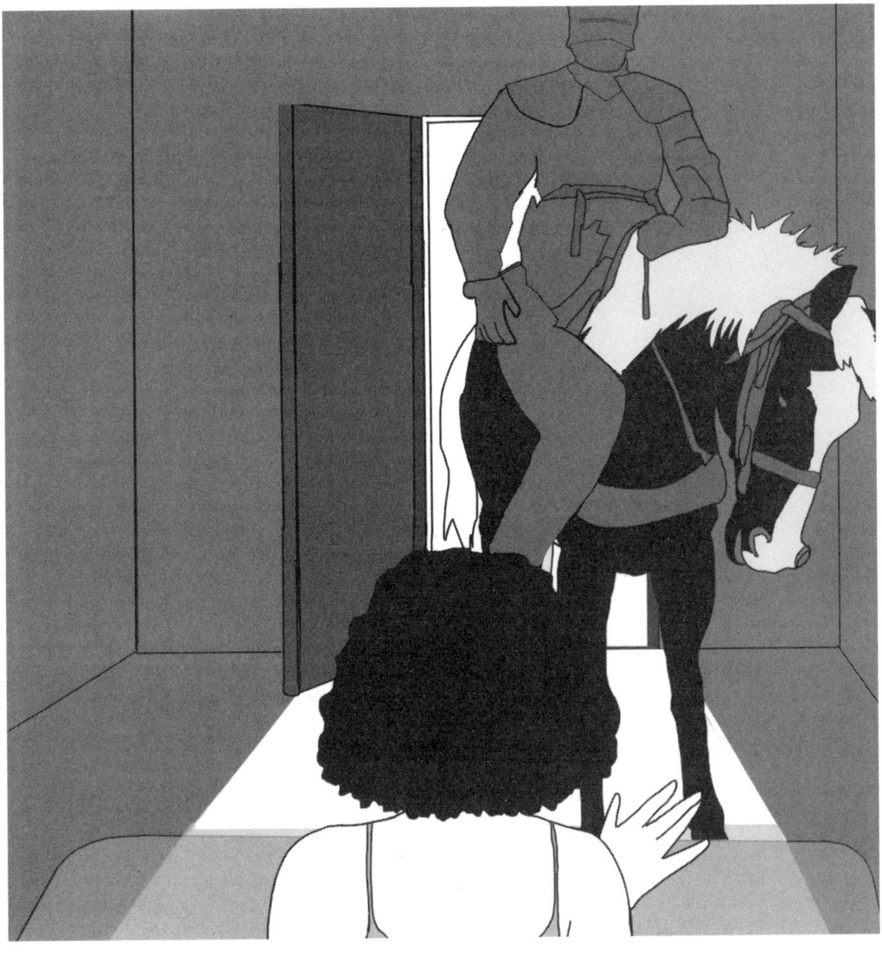

How to Know You've Found the One

So you've dated yourself and upped your level of self-care. You've tried and tested different dating techniques and gotten a good grasp on what you're looking for in a partner. You've even met a few people you think you might be compatible with! Surely you're more than ready for a relationship now?

The thing about dating someone is that the early stages often feel the best. Everything seems to be almost perfect. You find yourself charmed by

everything about your new romantic partner: their smile, the sound of their voice, their unique habits, the way they talk about things they are passionate about. You can imagine yourself spending forever with them, or at least a very long time. This is known as the honeymoon stage.

Frankly, all relationships start like this. The same goes for the moment a new parent first lays eyes on their newborn child. They're filled with love and curiosity as their body pumps the necessary hormones that enable them to bond with their offspring. We also get that "brand-new" feeling when starting pretty much anything that's supposed to bring us fulfillment—the first day of a new job, the first drive in a new car, the first night in a new apartment. But the initial excitement naturally plateaus and fades. This shouldn't put you off pursuing a relationship, however.

So why is it important to remember this when entering a new relationship? It's easy to misinterpret signs of compatibility when we're caught up in the rush of feelings that come at the beginning. This is an important time to look for green flags and red flags. These will vary for everyone, but here are some key things to look out for:

GREEN FLAGS	RED FLAGS
* Listens actively * Respects your boundaries * Shares your political/ religious views * Makes you like who you are around them * Conducts the relationship at a healthy pace	* Listens only to respond with something about themself * Overreacts when you say "no" * Holds political/religious views that clash with yours or perpetuate hate and violence against marginalized groups * Makes you feel like you can't fully be yourself around them * "Love bombs" you at the beginning, showering you with compliments, gifts, and attention, or acts distant and withholding, only giving you attention now and then

Knowing what green flags and red flags to look out for is key to ensuring a positive dating experience: you deserve to feel comfortable, trusting, and confident when entering a new relationship. I mean, after all this hard work to self-improve in preparation for a relationship, you deserve someone who recognizes this and is ready to treat you the way you treat yourself—and better!

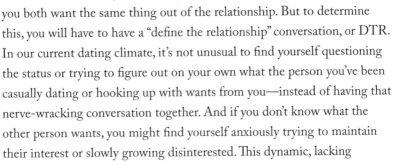

Them

My boundaries

One of the clearest signs that you've found someone with whom you are compatible is that you both want the same thing out of the relationship. But to determine this, you will have to have a "define the relationship" conversation, or DTR. In our current dating climate, it's not unusual to find yourself questioning the status or trying to figure out on your own what the person you've been casually dating or hooking up with wants from you—instead of having that nerve-wracking conversation together. And if you don't know what the other person wants, you might find yourself anxiously trying to maintain their interest or slowly growing disinterested. This dynamic, lacking communication, does not scream relationship material. Instead, take the risk and ask! Be direct. A person who is open about what they want at the beginning, who can confidently say that they are seeking companionship, and who demonstrates good communication skills is less likely to leave you guessing why they're sticking around. Choose the person who is interested in how you feel and who regularly expresses how you make them feel.

Knowing that not only are your new warm, fuzzy feelings reciprocated, but also that your partner wants to follow through on them is extremely important if you want to avoid finding yourself in an awkward unrequited romance situation. If you've ever been the recipient of unrequited feelings, you might remember feeling resistant, guilty, and maybe even a little frustrated that someone was more invested than you and expecting more than you were willing to give. Don't be that person. That doesn't mean you should suppress how you feel. What it does mean, however, is that you should always choose the person who is as excited about you as you are about them. You are, after all, someone worth getting excited about.

Finally, and most important of all, choose the person who makes you feel happy. It's really that simple. You deserve to be happy. You deserve to feel butterflies just thinking about someone. You deserve companionship that elicits positive feelings most of the time. This goes for family, friends, work, hobbies—everything. When you find the relationships that make you smile more, laugh more, dance more, relax more, and dream bigger, choose these relationships over and over again. In doing so, you're choosing yourself, the best choice you could ever make.

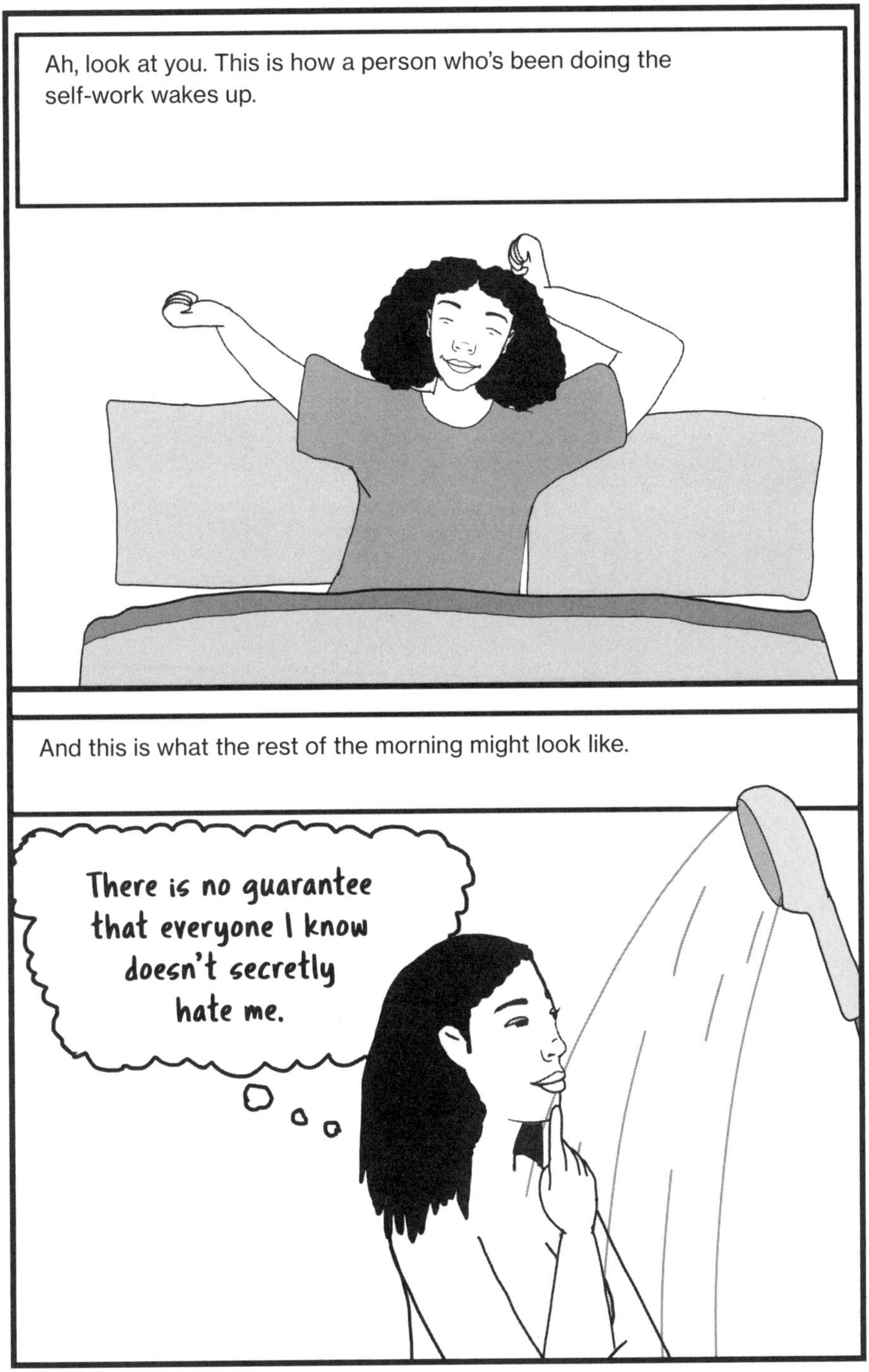
Ah, look at you. This is how a person who's been doing the self-work wakes up.
And this is what the rest of the morning might look like.
There is no guarantee that everyone I know doesn't secretly hate me.

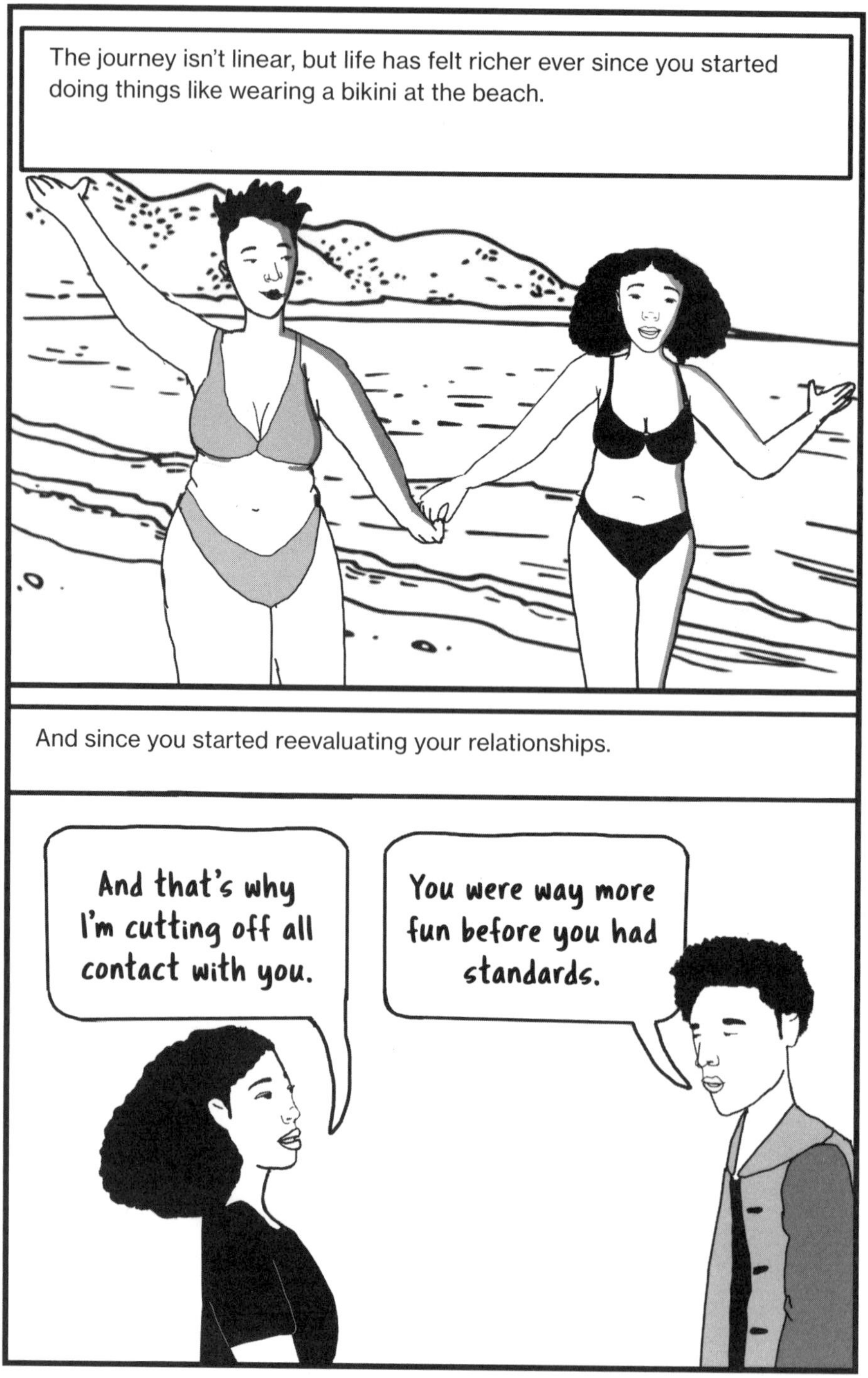
The journey isn't linear, but life has felt richer ever since you started doing things like wearing a bikini at the beach.
And since you started reevaluating your relationships.
And that's why I'm cutting off all contact with you.
You were way more fun before you had standards.

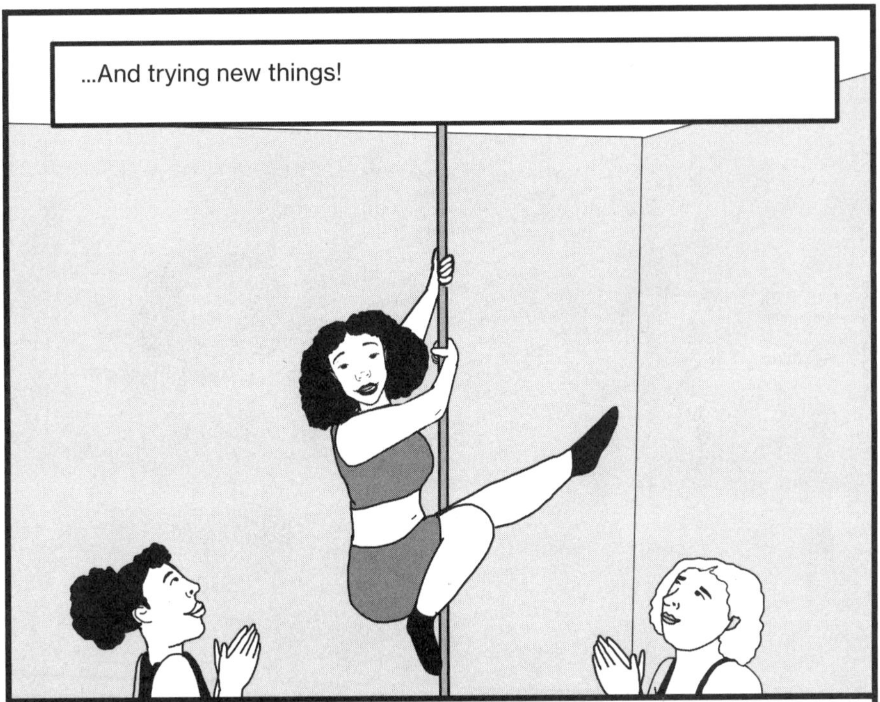
...And trying new things!

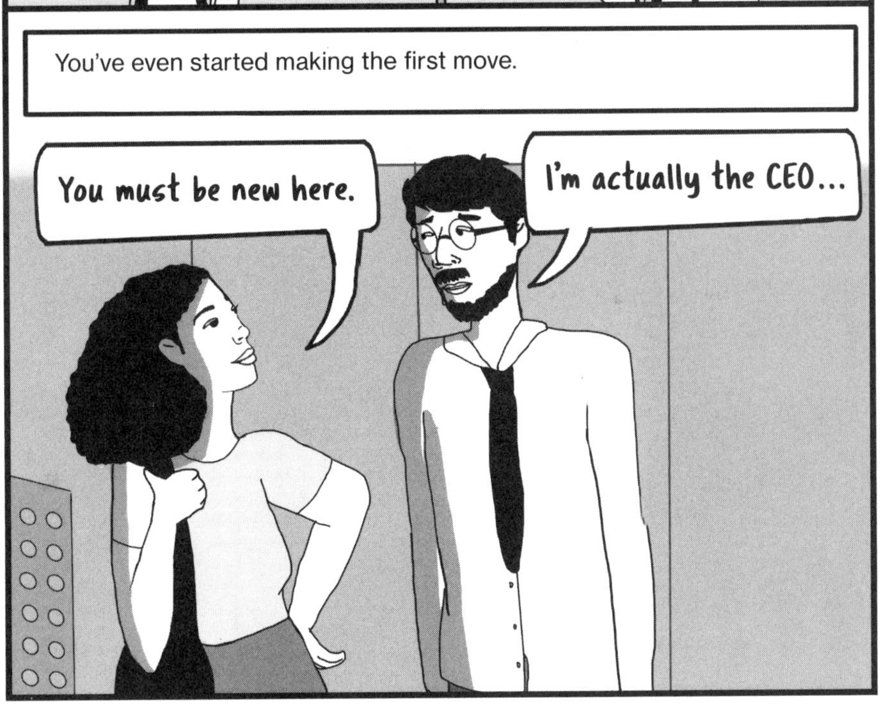
You've even started making the first move.
You must be new here.
I'm actually the CEO...

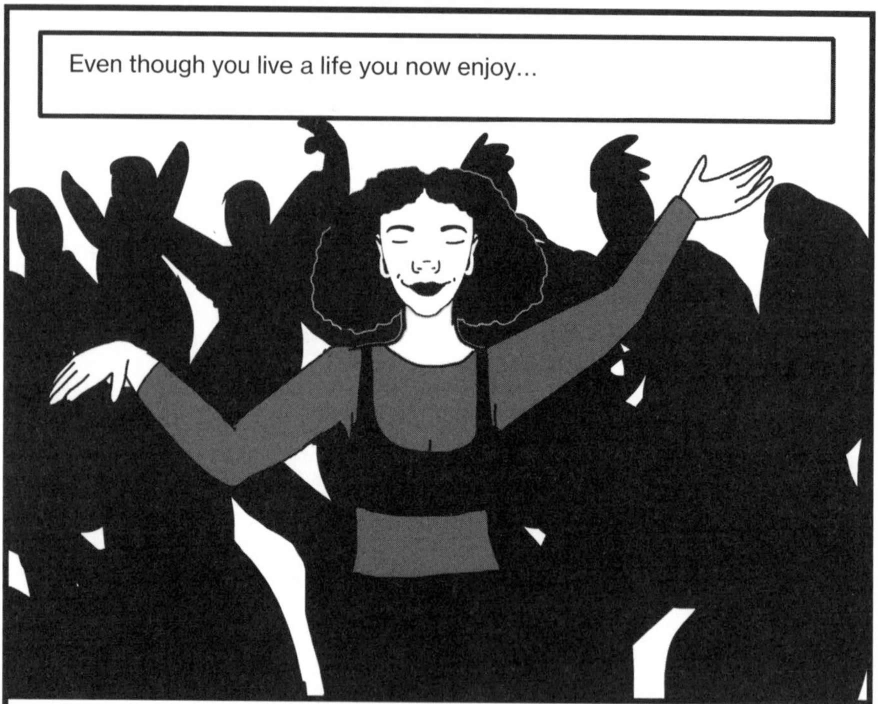
Even though you live a life you now enjoy...

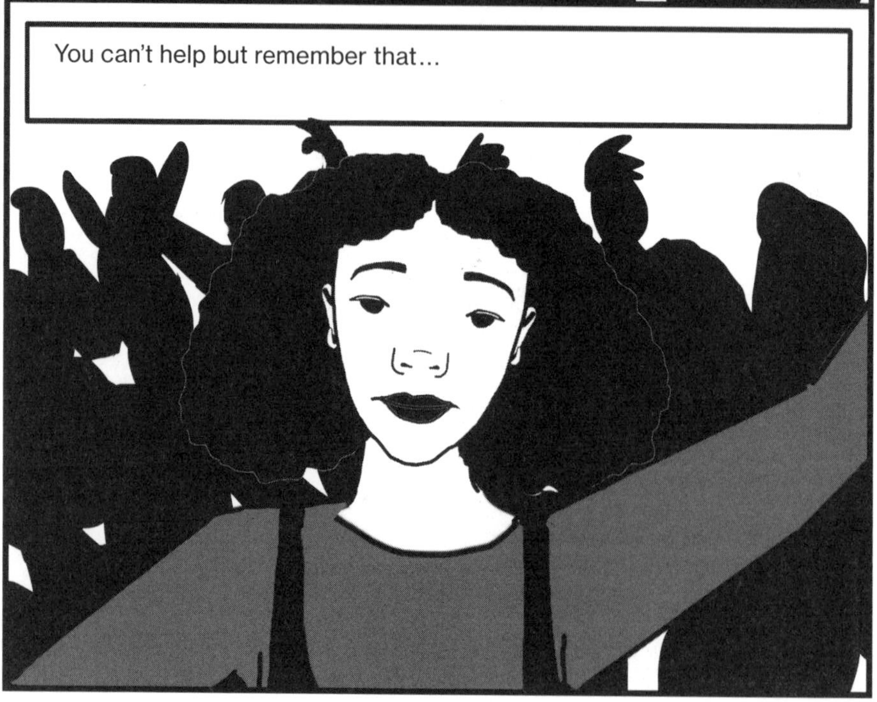
You can't help but remember that...

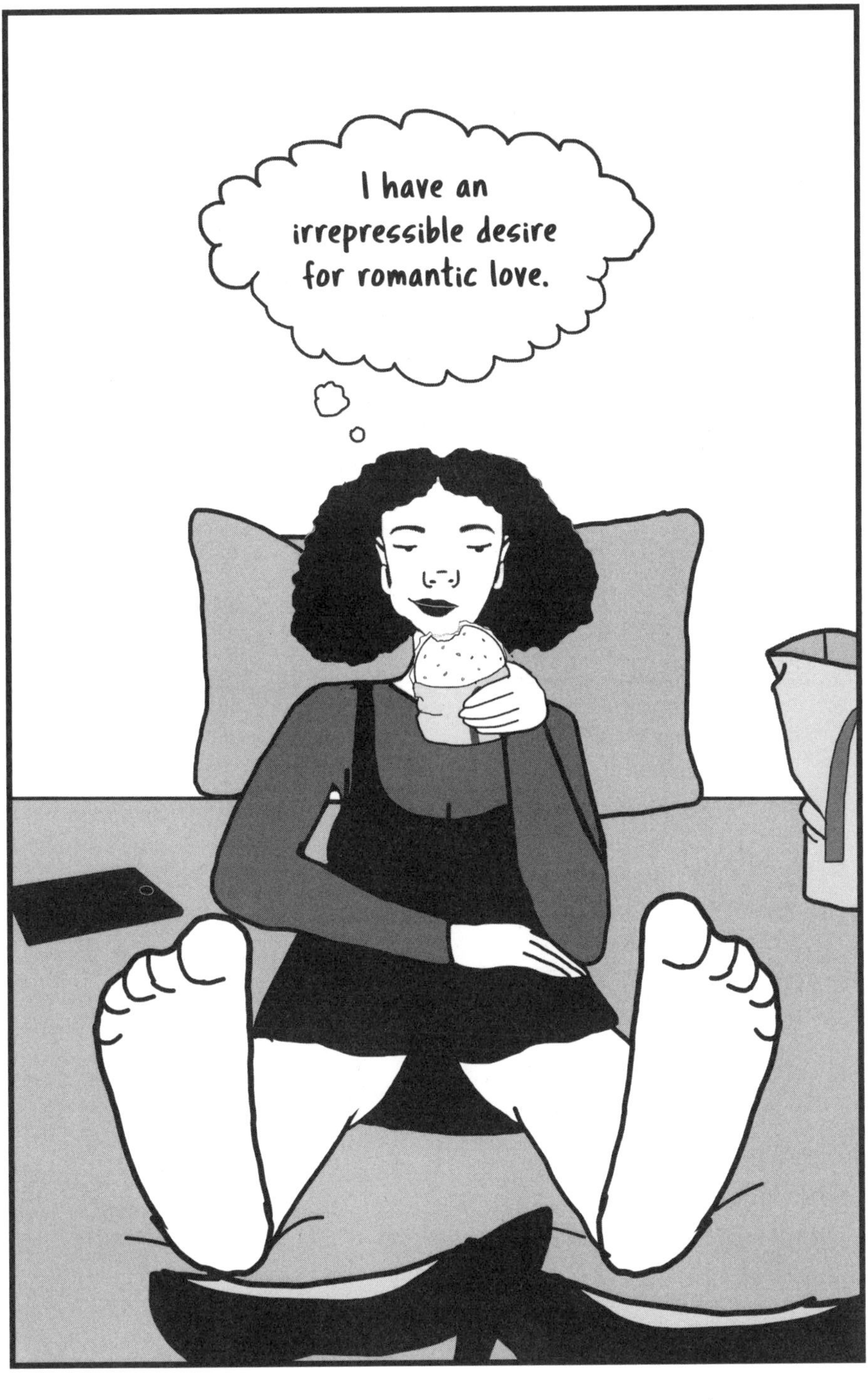
I have an irrepressible desire for romantic love.

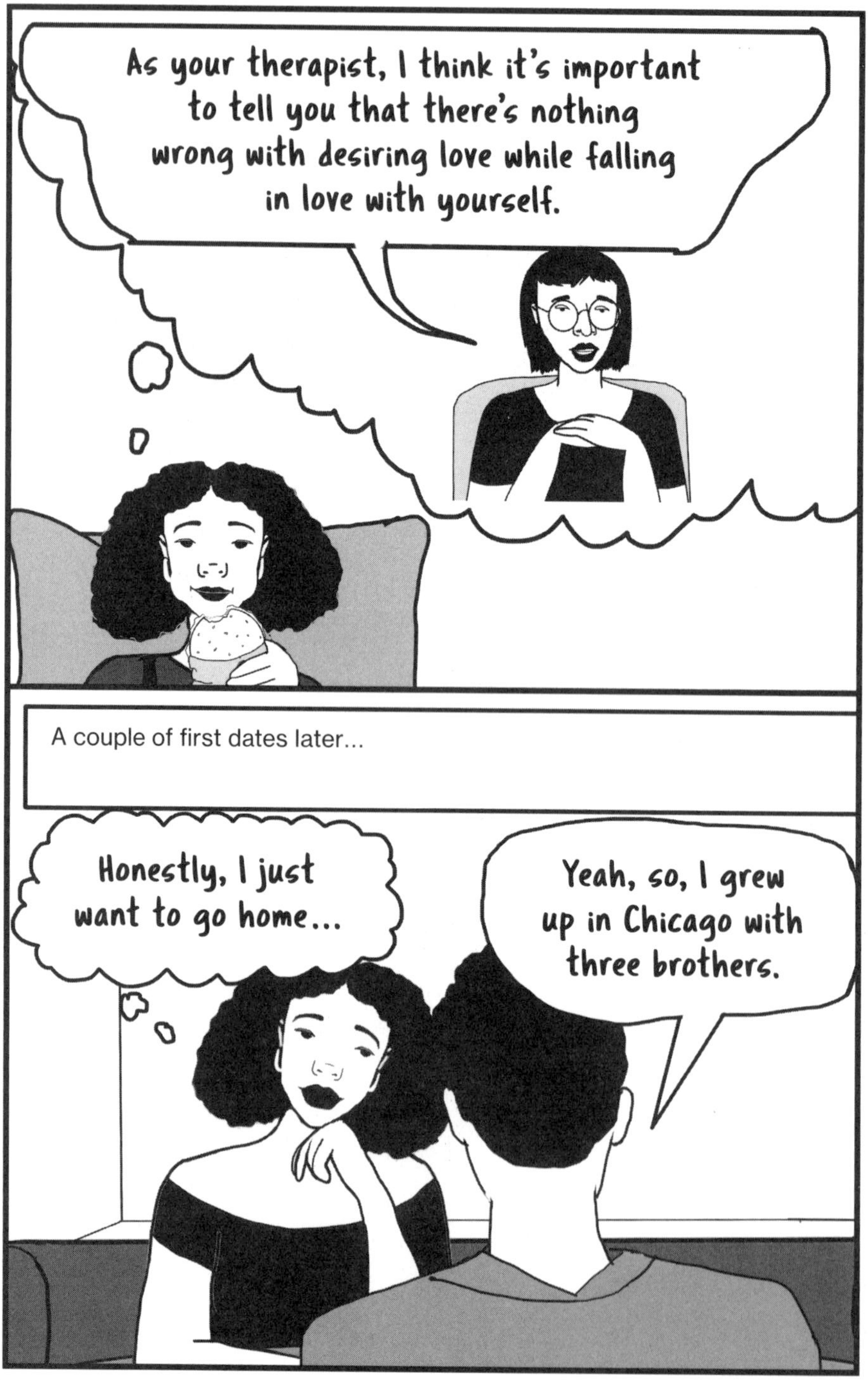
As your therapist, I think it's important to tell you that there's nothing wrong with desiring love while falling in love with yourself.
A couple of first dates later...
Honestly, I just want to go home...
Yeah, so, I grew up in Chicago with three brothers.

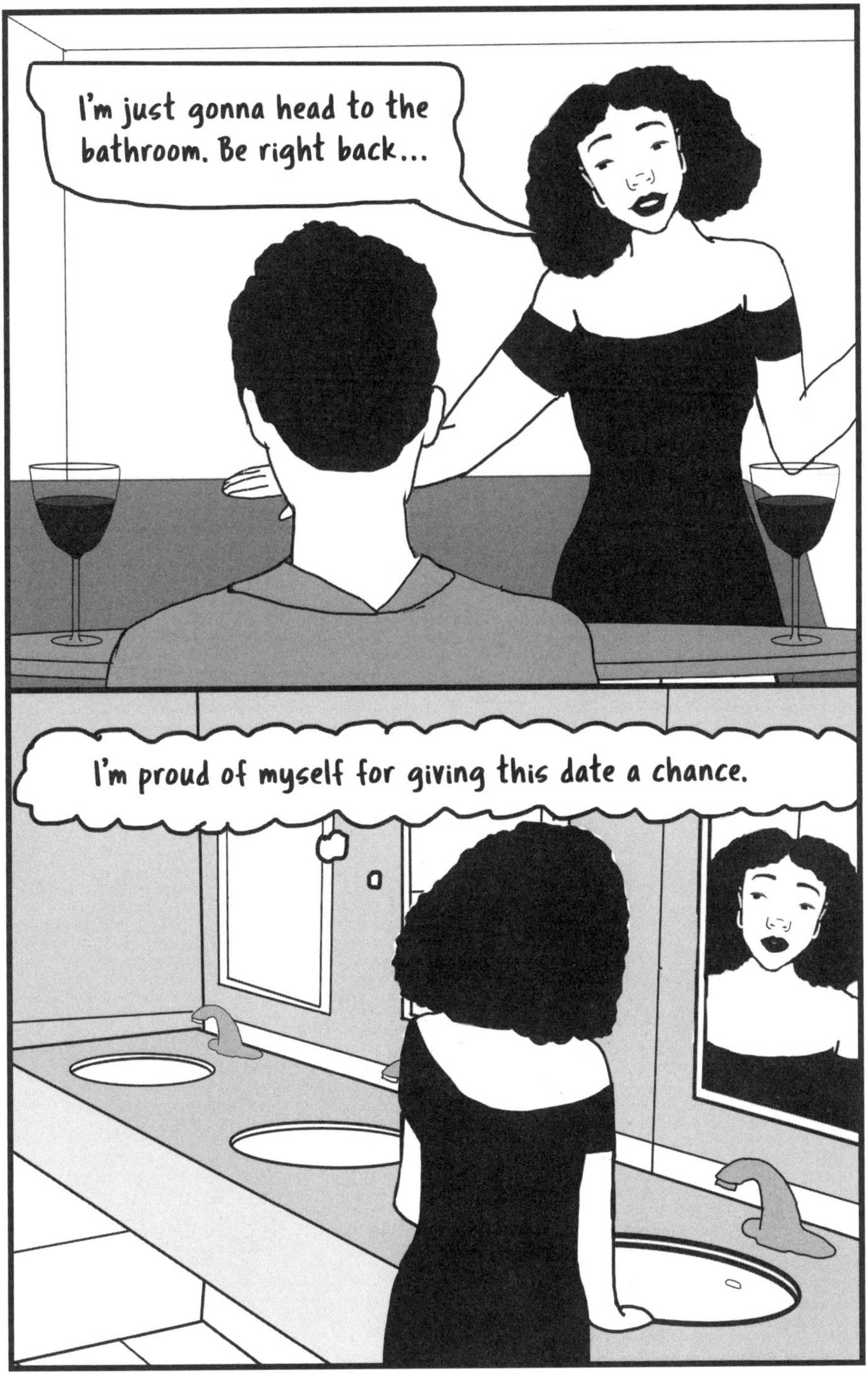
I'm just gonna head to the bathroom. Be right back...
I'm proud of myself for giving this date a chance.

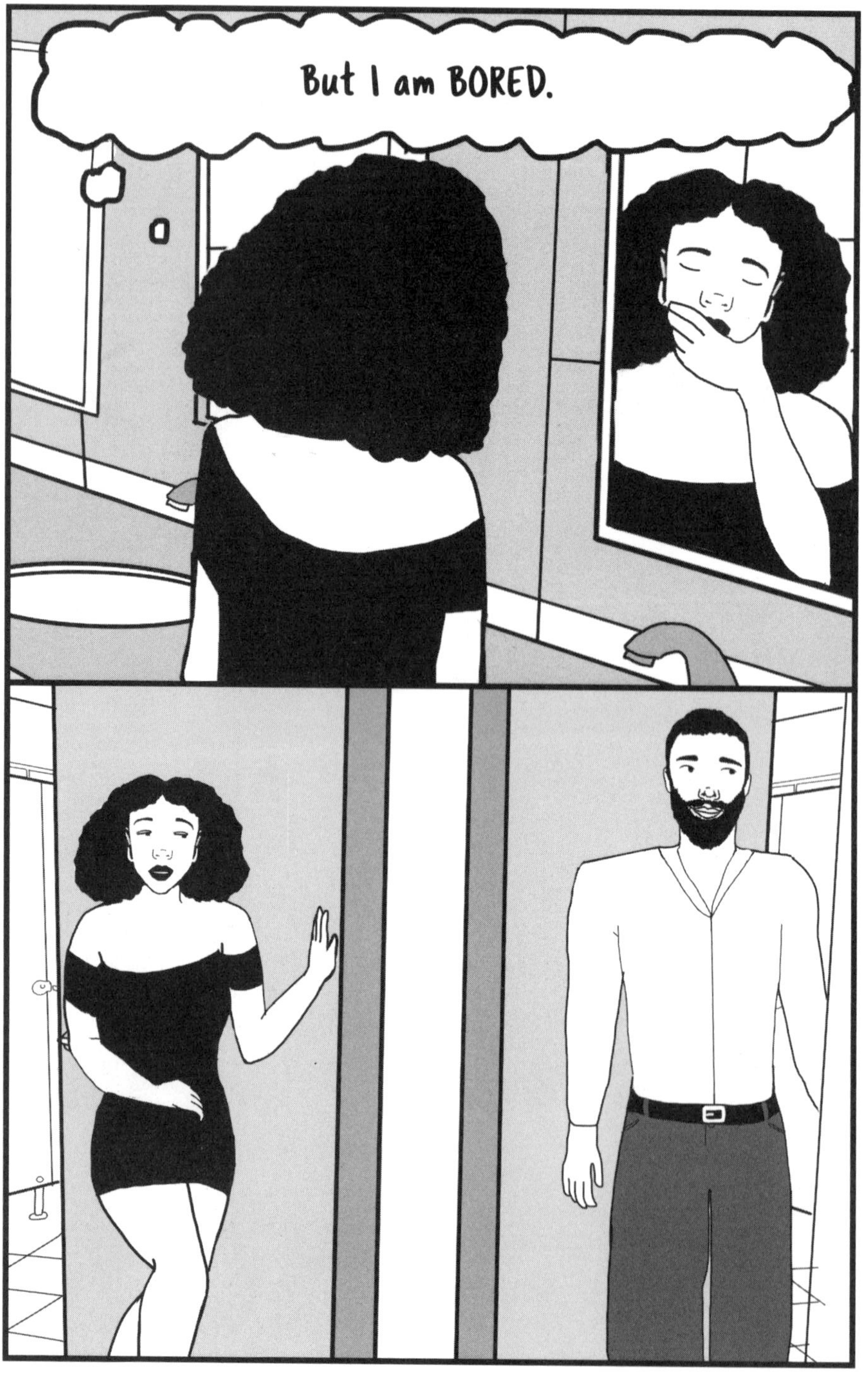
But I am BORED.

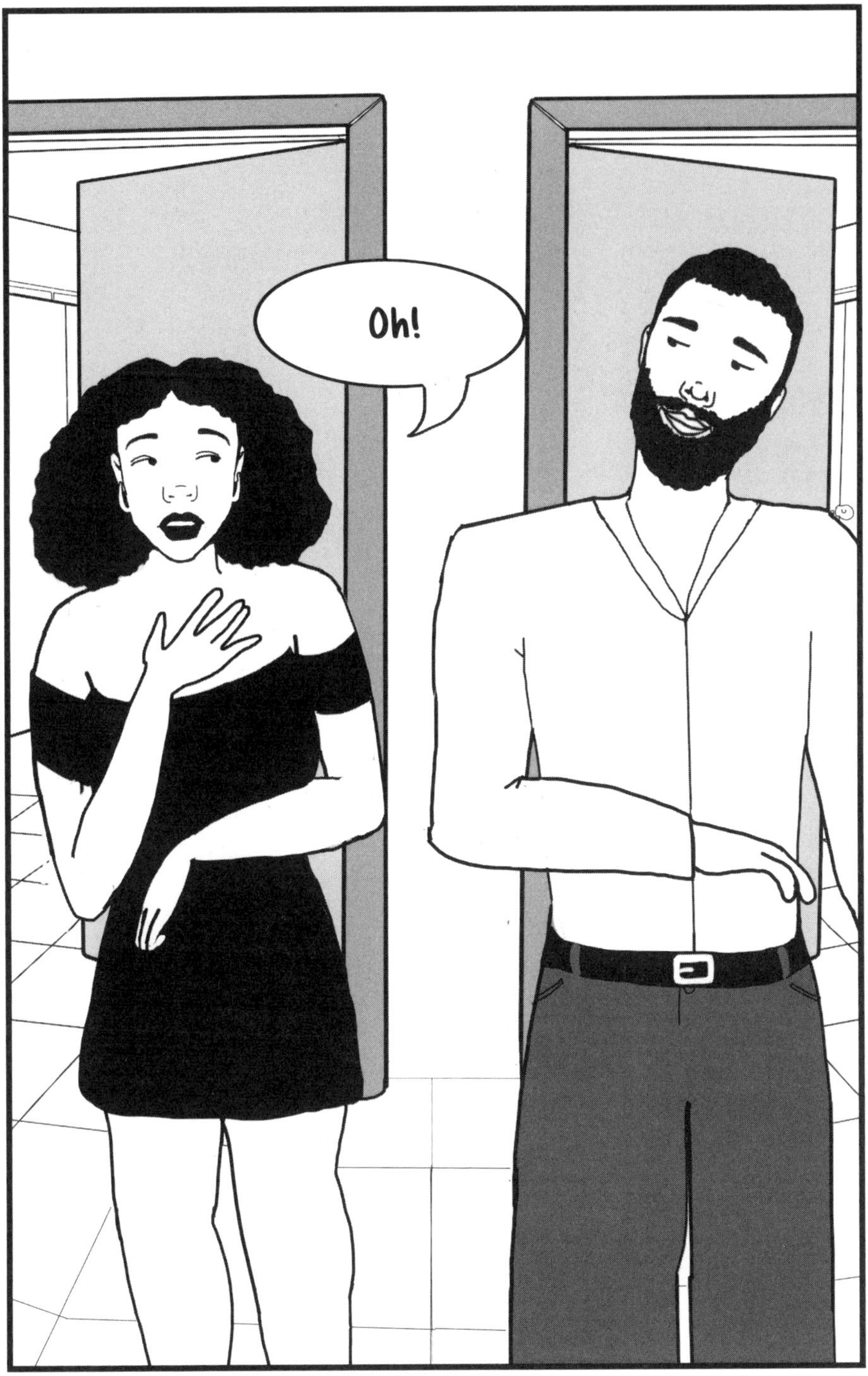
Oh!

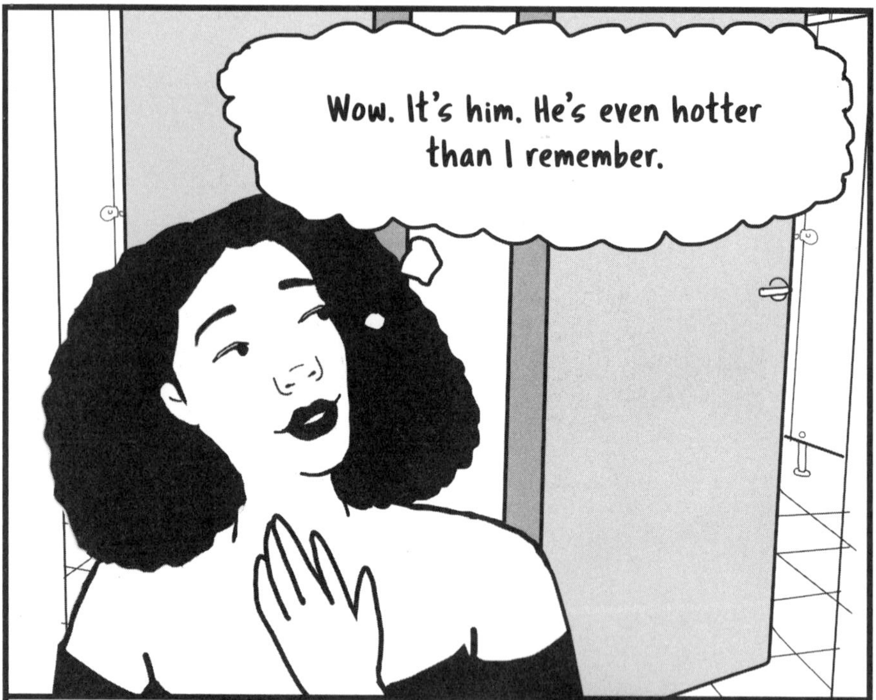
Wow. It's him. He's even hotter than I remember.

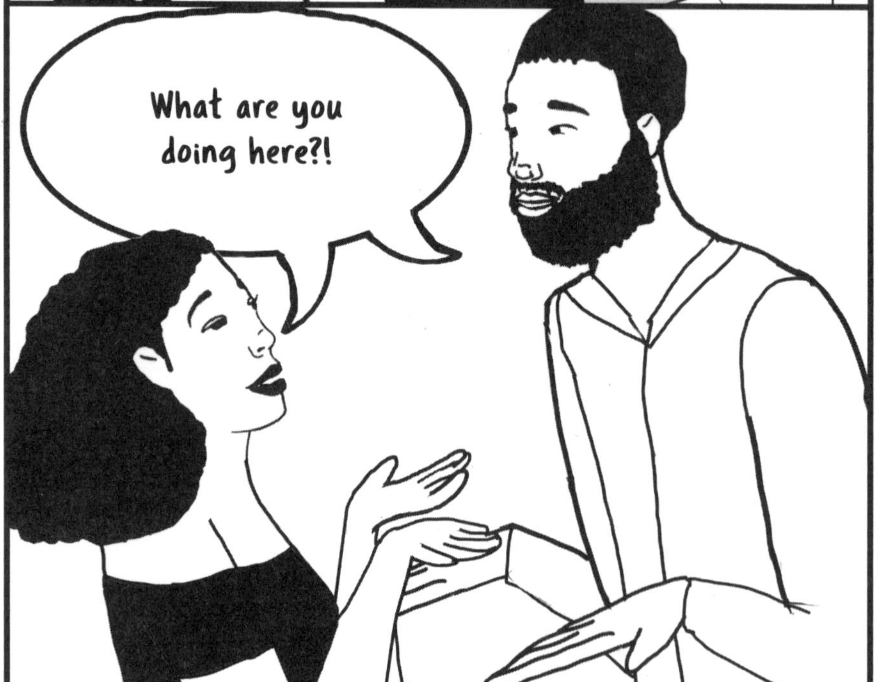
What are you doing here?!

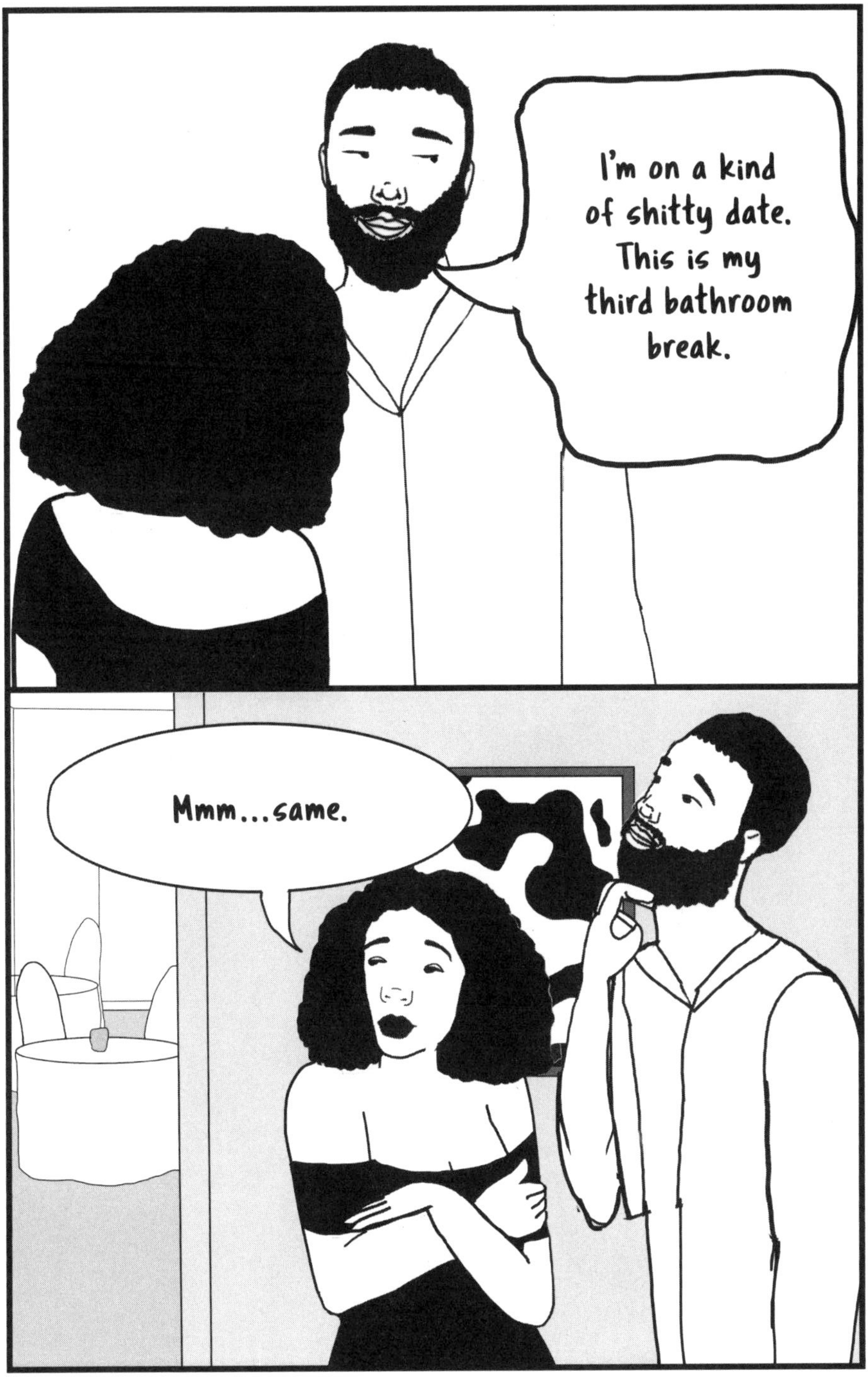
I'm on a kind of shitty date. This is my third bathroom break.
Mmm...same.

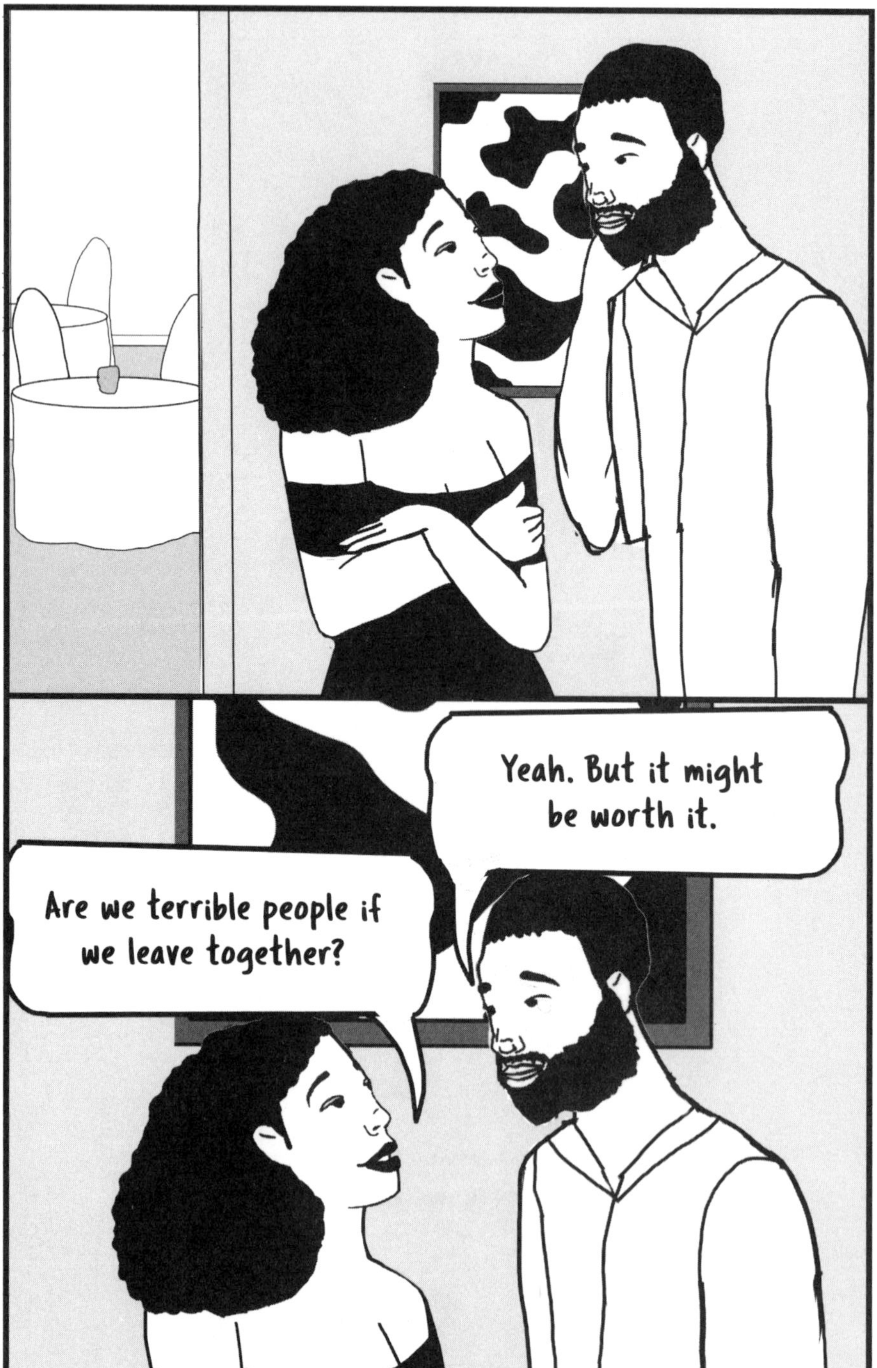
Are we terrible people if we leave together?
Yeah. But it might be worth it.

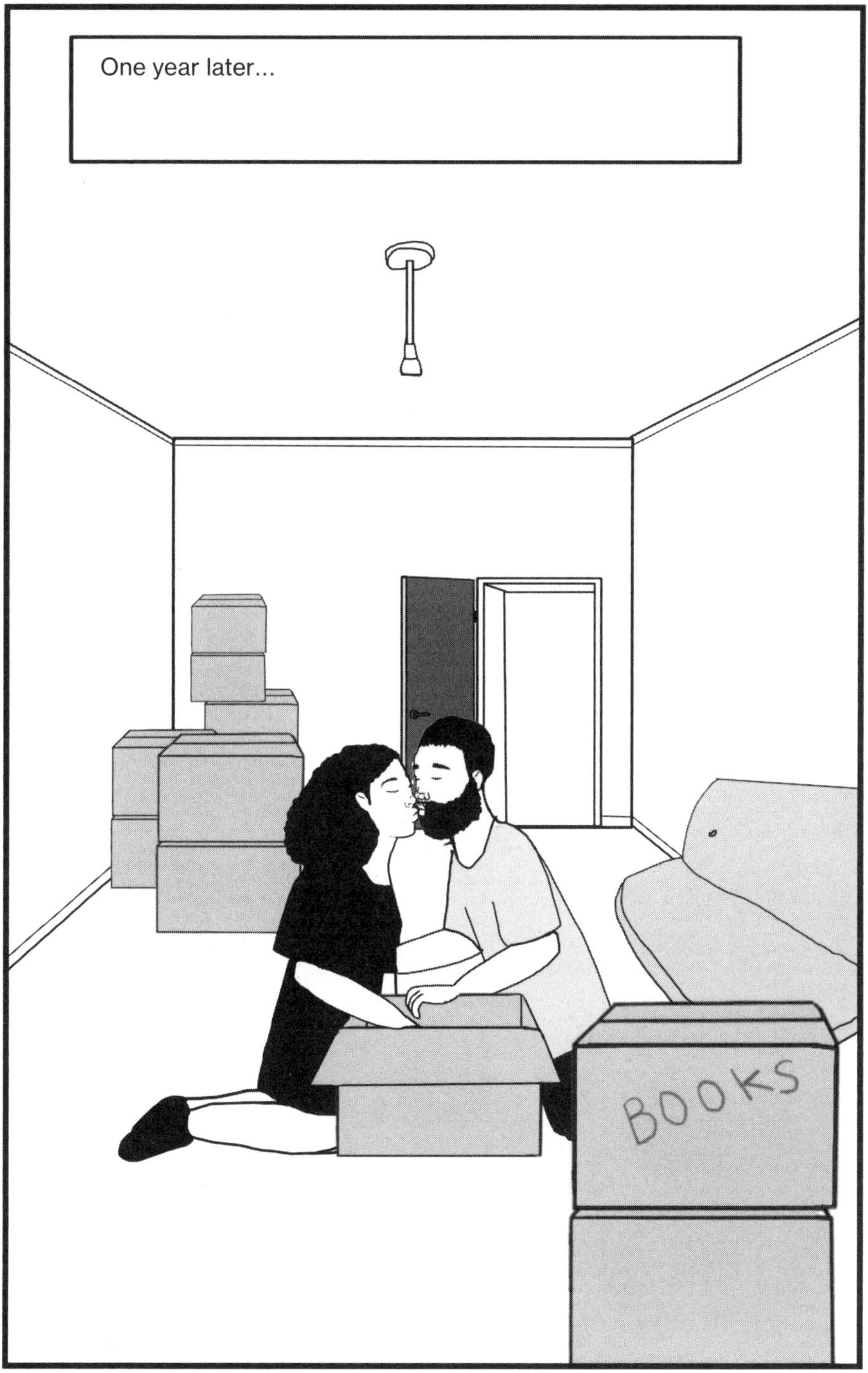
One year later...
BOOKS

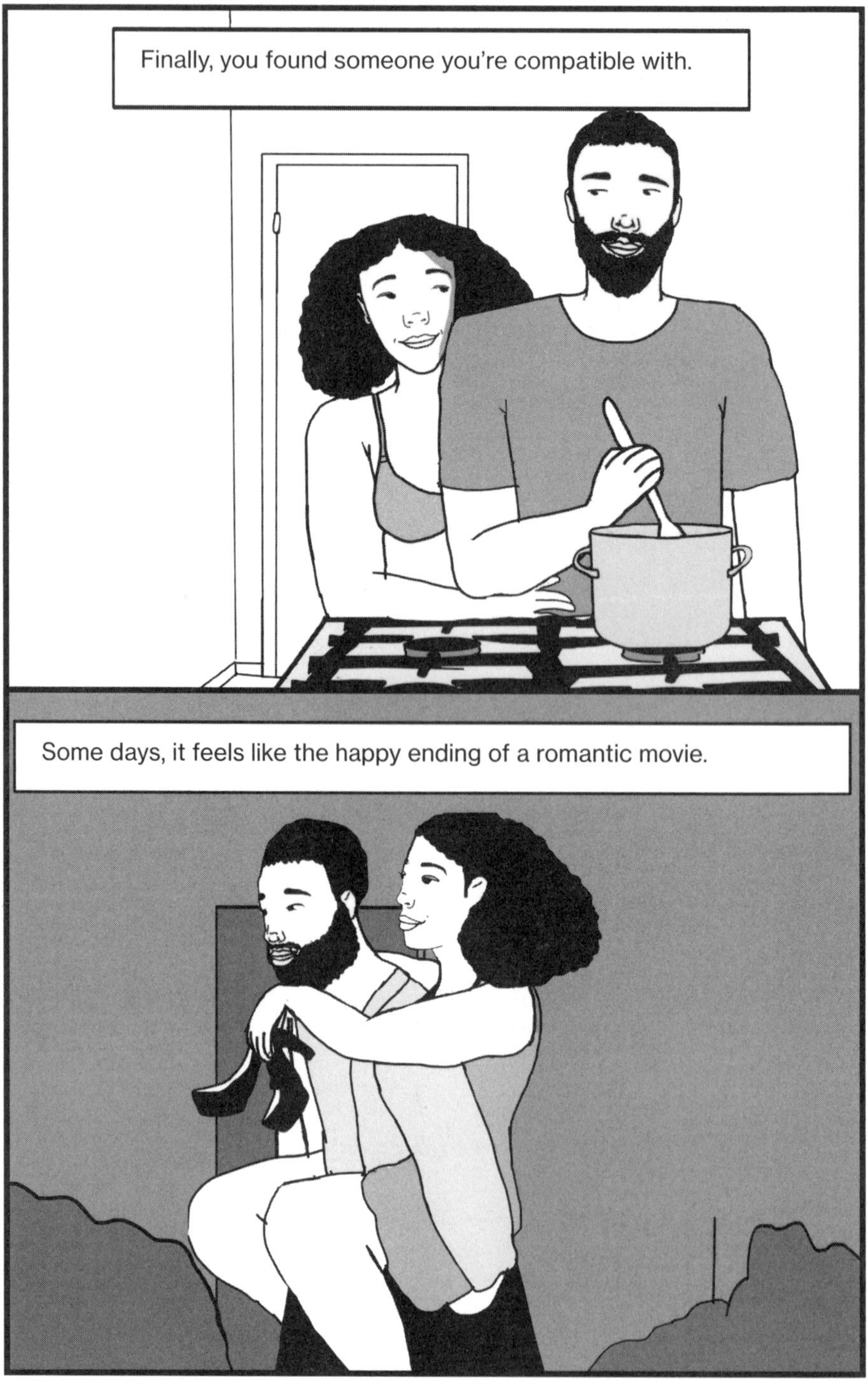
Finally, you found someone you're compatible with.
Some days, it feels like the happy ending of a romantic movie.

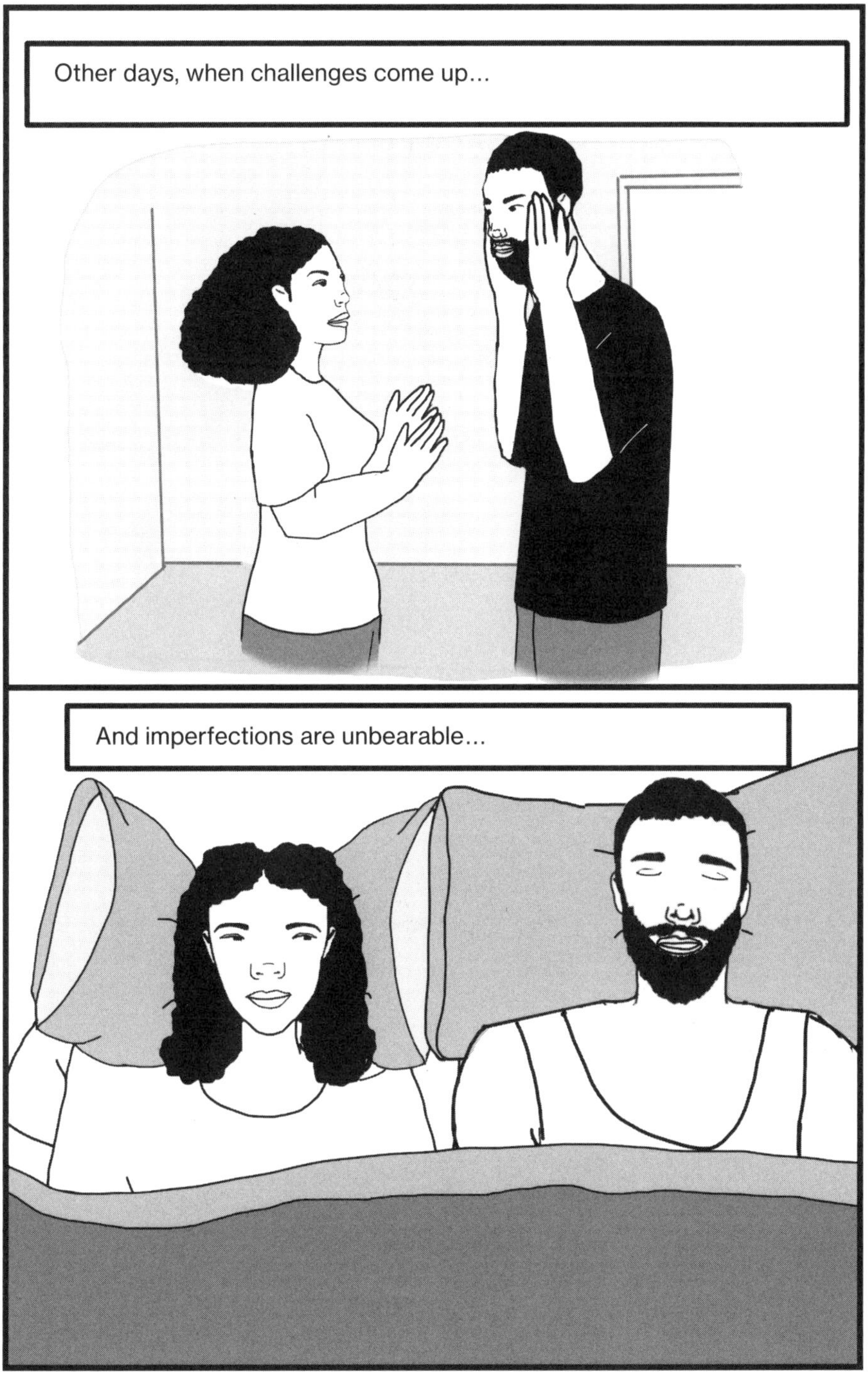
Other days, when challenges come up...
And imperfections are unbearable...

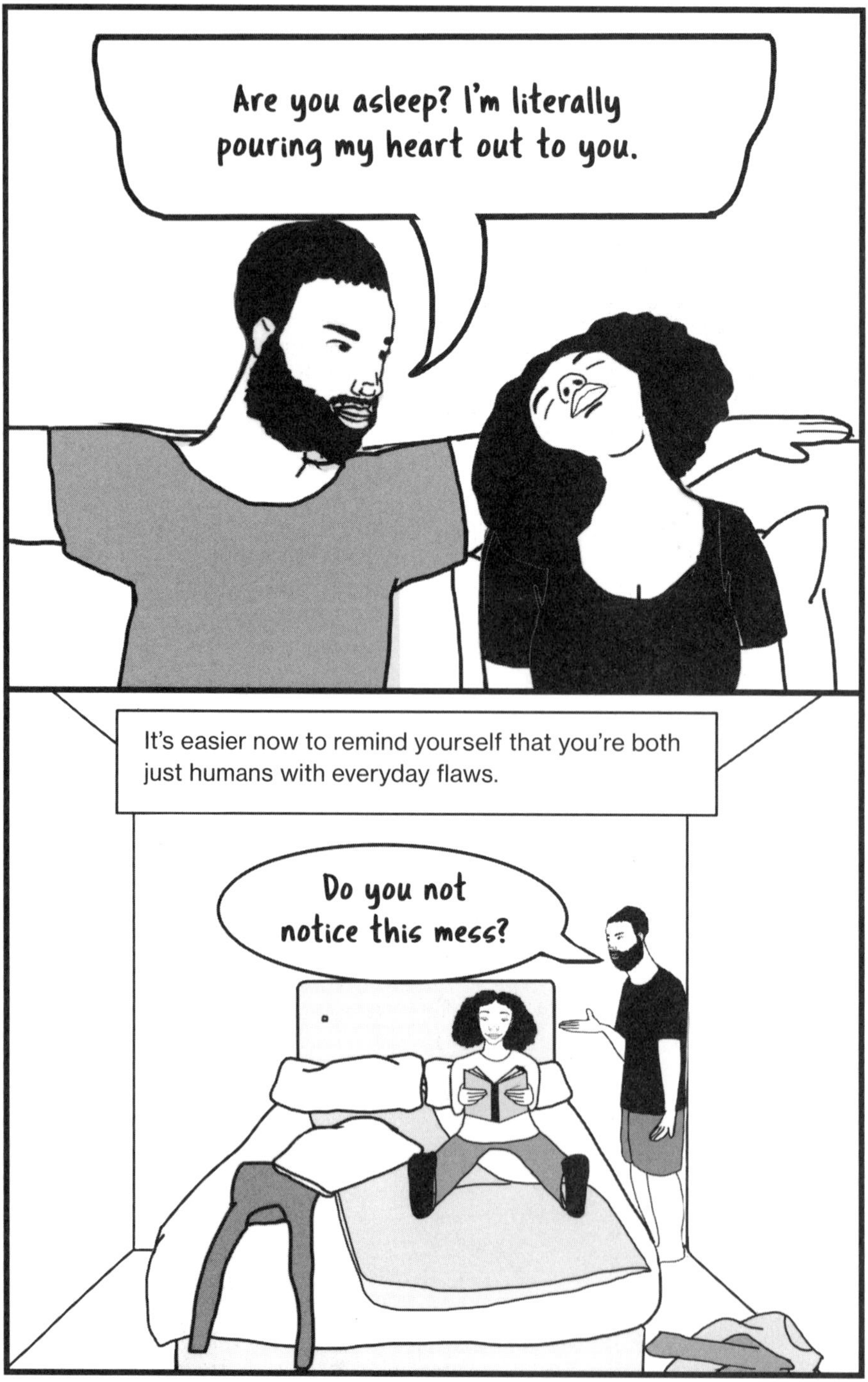
Are you asleep? I'm literally pouring my heart out to you.
It's easier now to remind yourself that you're both just humans with everyday flaws.
Do you not notice this mess?

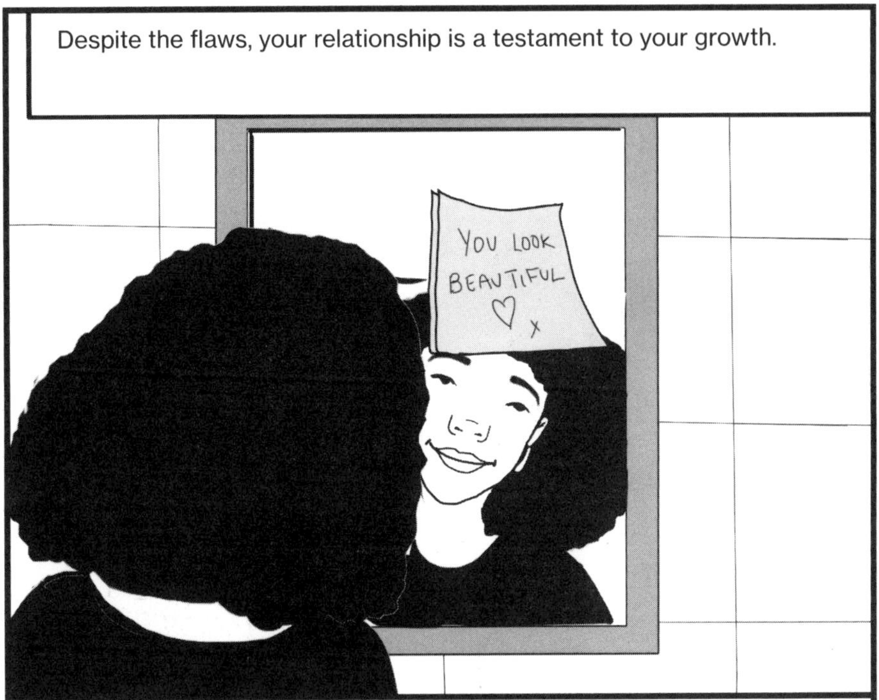
Despite the flaws, your relationship is a testament to your growth.
YOU LOOK BEAUTIFUL
x

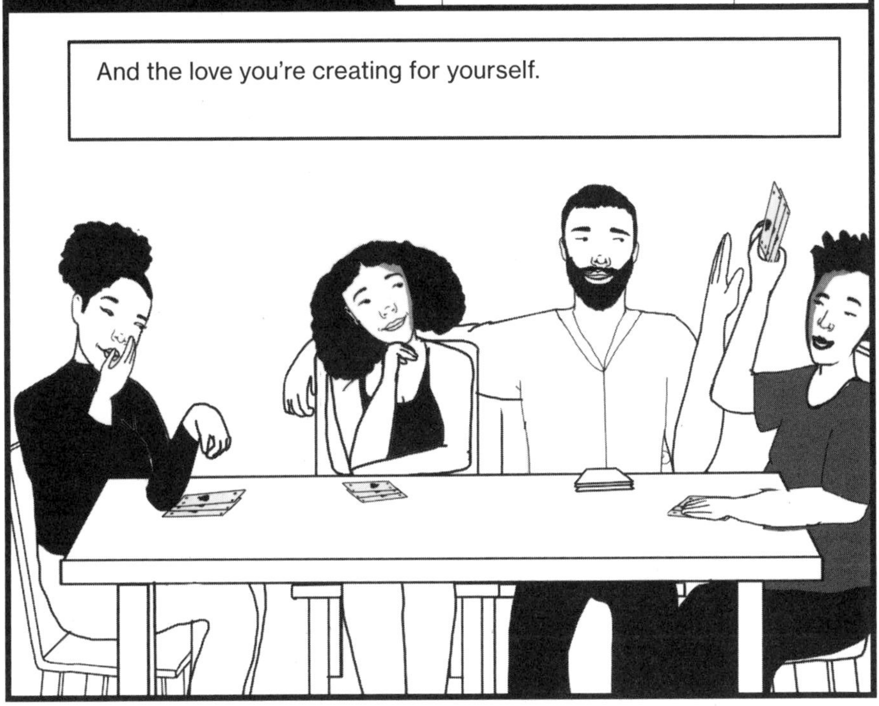
And the love you're creating for yourself.

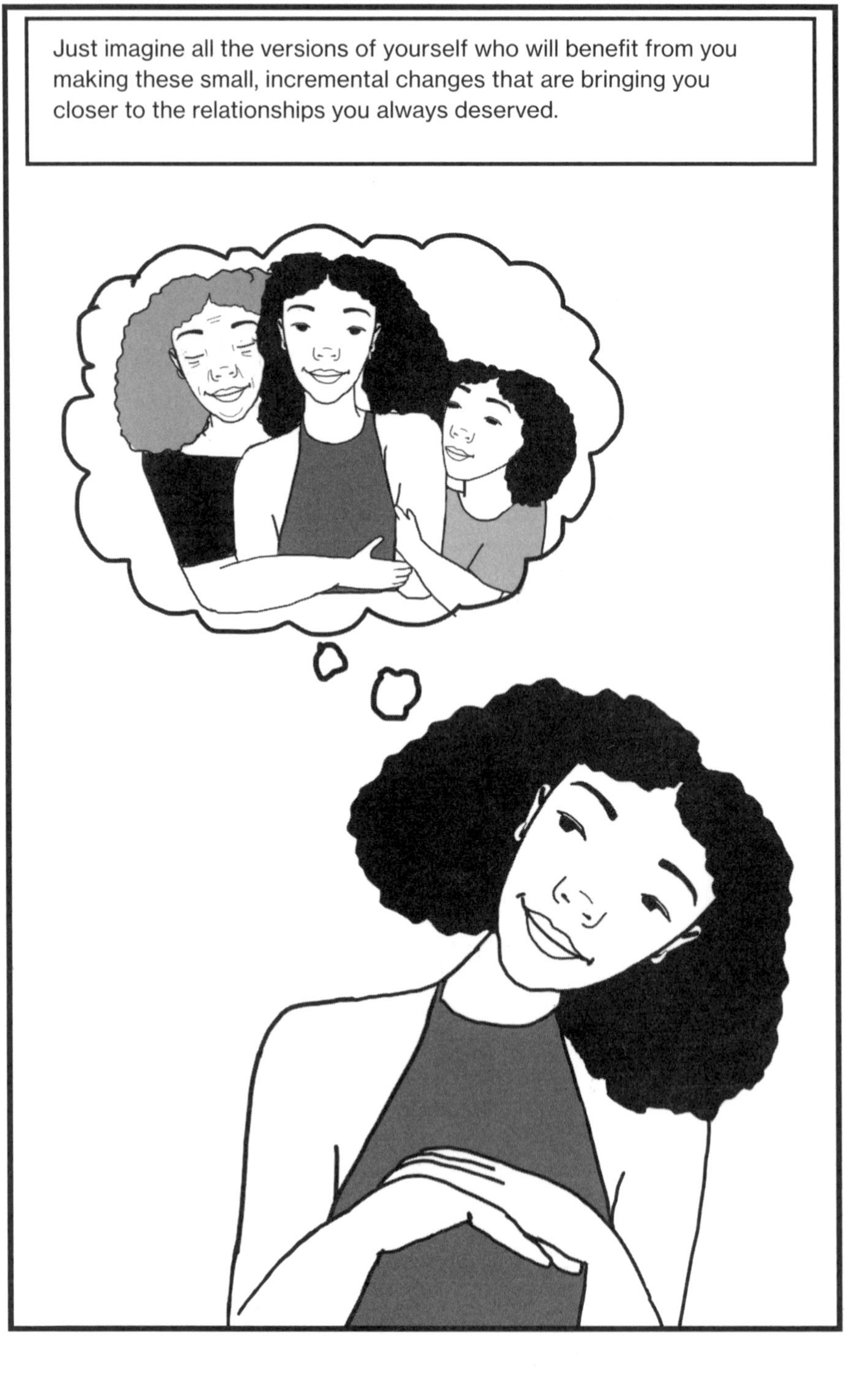
Just imagine all the versions of yourself who will benefit from you making these small, incremental changes that are bringing you closer to the relationships you always deserved.

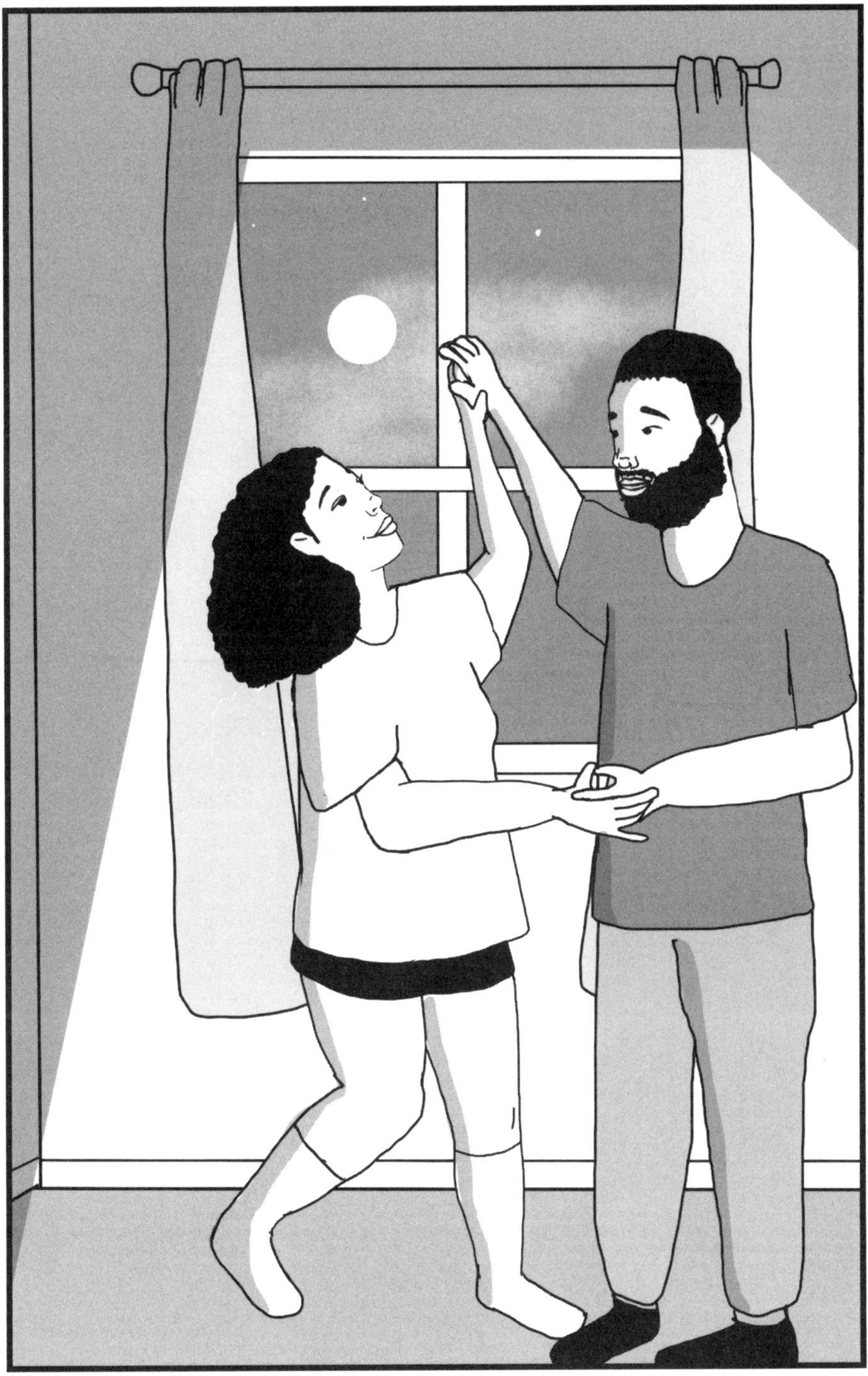

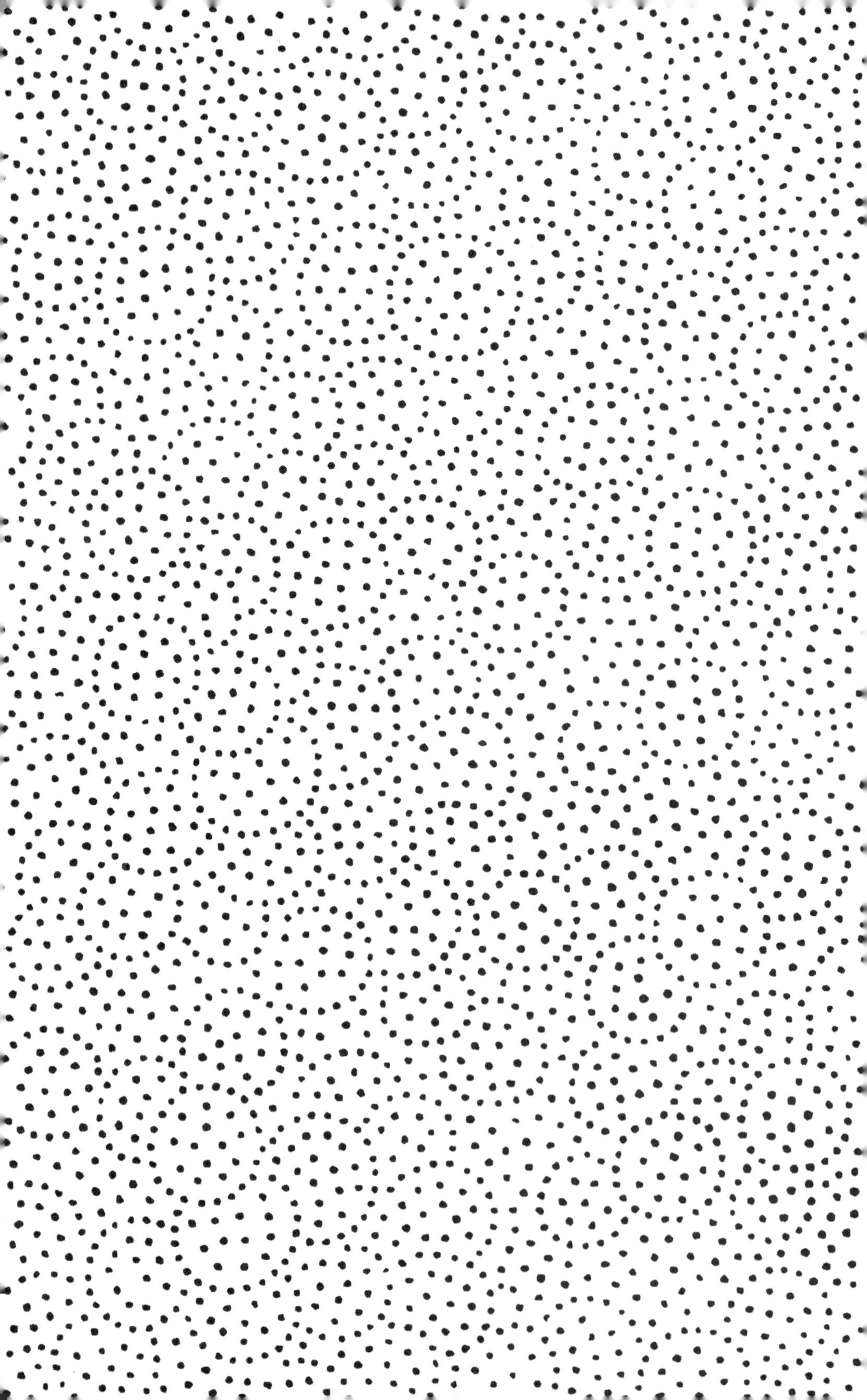

Acknowledgments

There are so many incredible people to thank for helping me reach this part of the book. The resilience, willpower, and motivation required for writing and illustrating a book are hard to muster without a solid support system. There are also those who acted as inspiration, some from the excruciating heartache they caused and others from the moments of true love and affection we got to share. The people I have the privilege of thanking here were all stepping stones in this journey.

Thank you to my mother for your extraordinary patience and encouragement when I moved back home and tried to start over. The pandemic took a lot from us—even more from you—but your faith that it gets better was unyielding and the magic ingredient that got me through. I love you always!

To my siblings, you are my very best friends and I could never thank you enough. Throughout, you guys have generously extended your support, honesty, and wisdom, which were pivotal for my creative process. Your thoughts and criticism are more important to me than anyone's and it lifts my spirit every time you're proud of me. Thank you, Tunrola, Akin, and Feyi for being the best siblings anyone could ask for.

To my cousins, especially Kayode and Esther, thank you for just being there. Both of you have had front-row seats to many of my love stories and some of the most humiliating times in my life. Regardless, you've always observed without judgment. You guys teach me to brush it off, rise up, and love again. Without these reminders I would have nothing to share in this book. I love you guys!

To my beautiful friends, old and new, this book is for you, by you, and written with you in spirit. Thank you for listening to the long, tearful voice notes and grumpy phone calls, for the coffee dates, the dinner dates, the long hugs, the sleepovers, and the constant reminders from each of you that I'm worthy, no matter how much I'd insist I wasn't. My heart is in one piece because of you. Thank you, Pamela, Harriet, Adaeze, Anisah, and Marge. I love you all so much.

Thank you to everyone at the *New Yorker* magazine, in particular the cartoon editors Emma Allen and Colin Stokes. Without you guys recognizing my comic *Oyin and Kojo*, I wouldn't be where I am today. Thank you for seeing me and offering me a seat at such a prestigious table. I truly can't thank you enough.

To everyone at Ayesha Pande Literary Agency and Anjali and Kayla, you've been an incredible support system and have advocated for me and fueled my motivation for this book from the beginning to the end. Thank you for helping me realize my worth and for the immense amount of work you've put into this process. I hope for many more projects together!

To my wonderful editor at Princeton Architectural Press, Kristen Hewitt, thank you for your patience, brilliance, creativity, and genuine support through this whole process. I started out as a new cartoonist with the hope of one day creating a book in the distant future, and you helped to bring that vision into my current reality. I appreciate you so much!

To the design team at Princeton Architectural Press, thank you so much for meticulously bringing this book to life. It wouldn't be what it is without your skill and creativity. You've played such a major role in this whole process, and I'm eternally grateful.

Thank you to publicity and marketing at PA Press, Wes Seeley and Jessica Tackett, for your enthusiasm, strategy, and faith in this book. Without you guys, this book may not have landed in the hands of those who need it! All your work is very much appreciated.

To all the loves, crushes, and infatuations who inspired this book, I'm extremely grateful to each and every one of you. Knowing all of you was knowing myself at different stages of my life. Through every relationship, I grow a little more compassionate, self-aware, and wise in the knowledge that the love of my life exists in so many. Thank you to the ones who made my world more colorful for at least six months and then to the ones who drained the color when they left. This book is yours, too.

Finally, an enormous thank you to you, the reader. Our love lives can be a huge tangled mess that takes a lot of time to make sense of, but everyone deserves to enjoy theirs. It's an honor to share what I've learned about love and dating with you. Thank you for picking up this book, and most importantly, thank you for allowing my words and creativity to inspire your own love story.

Sarah Akinterinwa is a British cartoonist, illustrator, and writer. She started her career in 2020, during the first lockdown of the COVID-19 pandemic, by creating the comic *Oyin and Kojo*, which now features in the *New Yorker*. Her work explores dating, relationships, identity, politics, and navigating adult life as a young woman of color.

Published by
Princeton Architectural Press
A division of Chronicle Books LLC
70 West 36th Street
New York, New York 10018
papress.com

Printed and bound in Canada
26 25 24 23 4 3 2 1 First edition

Editor: Kristen Hewitt
Design concept: Sarah Akinterinwa
Design and typesetting: Paul Wagne

Library of Congress Cataloging-in-Publicatic
Names: Akinterinwa, Sarah, author, artist.
Title: Why you'll never find the one : and why it doesn't matter / Sarah
Other titles: Why you will never find the one
Description: First edition. | New York : Princeton Architectural Press, [2023] |
Summary: "An illustrated dating guide rooted in cartoonist Sarah Akinterinwa's experi
as a millennial Black woman, that encourages readers to be introspective, honest, and practical in their love lives"—Provided by publisher.
Identifiers: LCCN 2022037818 | ISBN 9781797222530 (paperback) | ISBN 9781797224213 (ebook)
Subjects: LCSH: Dating (Social customs)—Comic books, strips, etc. | Courtship—Comic books, strips, etc. | Mate selection—Comic books, strips, etc. | Interpersonal relations—Comic books, strips, etc.
Classification: LCC HQ801 .A52177 2023 | DDC 646.7/7—dc23/eng/20220824
LC record available at https://lccn.loc.gov/2022037818